HOW CHAI TEA IS MADE

HOW CHAI TEA IS MADE

Sutichai Savathasuk

How Chai Tea is Made
© 2023 Sutichai Savathasuk
ISBN: 979-8-9892280-0-3 (paperback)
ISBN: 979-8-9892280-1-0 (ebook)

Cover art, "How Chai Tea is Made"
© 2022 Nicholas Dobkin

First Edition, 2023

Printed in the United States of America

Cover Design by Nicholas Dobkin
Layout Design by Elena Mussari-Fugate
Interior Drawings by John Park
Chapter Artwork by Ashley Lam

Quotes About the Author by Totally Real People

"He is the most fearless artist I have ever met."
~ Ariel Jimenez

"Chai is incredibly brave. He jumps head-first into the unknown without a single flinch. He improvises and adapts until he has the audience in the palm of his hand, whether that's onstage or in everyday life."
~ Jaclyn Lee Yangyuen

"Chai is a man of many modes: friend— engineer— creative eclectic— journeying heart— boba enthusiast— terrible pun lover— and now, published author, and a damn good one at that.

What you may not yet fully realize is that the tome you now hold in your hands is not just a collection of colorful poems, amusing anecdotes, and thoughtful reflections on life, but a carefully crafted portrayal of everything this man lives and breathes... or at least what could feasibly fit in one volume.

Chai is a masterful storyteller and a virtuoso in vivid depiction, threading that ever so delicate balance between the hilarious and heartfelt. This truly is his magnum opus and a clear precursor of even greater work to come."
~ Christian Perfas, author of *Play: A Reclamation of Soul*

"He's aight."
~ Cheog, younger brother

"I thought this book was going to be about boba- I was wrong..."
~ Kris, elder brother

"He's the most okayest guy I know."
~ Kendra Sazon

"Why would you write a book so good that it makes me cry?"
~ Bebo

"He is so handsome."
~ all the grandmas

"Willing to endure difficult obstacles and challenges especially with good friends. Also capable of eating 2 lbs of Sour Patch and then some."
~ Jose Herrera

"Down for an adventure even before he knows what it is."
~ Gabriella de Asis, author of *Coming Home*

"Sure, why not."
~ James Quan, upon being asked to give a quote

"You foo."
~ Yinfung Khong

"You're, like, a nerdicle genius."
~ Aurora Blessing Basco

"Chai is an exqusite jellyfish."
~ VOTH (Voice of the Harbor)

"Mr. Chai Tea is a wordsmith wizard with infinite ink to make you think. His poetry is rooted in wordplay intellect, courageous honesty, pure authenticity, and a loving gulp of silly."
~ Alex Petunia, author of *Tending My Wild*

"To experience Chai's work is to witness to an ever-evolving process. Watching him develop and unfold his perception of the world is nothing short of remarkable. One never knows what or how he will reveal his inner mechanics, but when he does, he delivers every time."
~ Arianna "Lady" Basco

Table of Contents

PREFACE

Greetings brave wanderer, intrigued spirit, lost soul,

my name is Chai, like your favorite drink,
unless you prefer coffee, or booze, then that's okay, too.

Whoever you may be, you hold my life in your hands.
This book is my history, in the hopes that you get something out of sharing this adventure with me. I believe
you will enjoy the contents in these pages, and if you
don't, then thank you for your support and no refunds.

At the very core, I'm a nerd and an adventurer, as we all
are some kind of curiosity and some kind of wisdom.

The people I introduce in these pages
are neither heroes nor villains,
but simply humans
who affected
my journey.

These are my truths.
I suppose what I'm saying is...

*To life – The ultimate desire is making our own purpose. We
are the masters of our destiny. Make the most of your limited
time here and live. Know that you are worthy with no one to
tell you otherwise.*

**Or not, life can suck,
And that's ok too... probably, maybe... I don't know.
Just keep living,
and don't stop
unless it's for rest.**

Enjoy.

STEP I: GROWING TEA LEAVES

Childhood was wack.
I had some pretty good snacks
sprinkled with trauma.

"The tea leaves are ripe and ready for harvest."

Scoops of Green

Occasions to celebrate
are fleeting, savored for nostalgia.

Little me was treated to
the all-you-can-eat seafood buffet.

The adults nodded off, my
screaming, background fodder.

It was the joy of running wild
with layers of dishes stacked,

overflowing with crawfish,
lobster claws lining my arm

like a server, delivering sashimi,
handrolls, and shumai to my

insatiable appetite / craved
for more, saved a space for desserts.

My choice, was the encore,
that verdant beauty at the end of the line.

And I discovered
green tea ice cream.

This dairy I hadn't had daily
greatly brought glee to my belly.

On mundane days, droughts of flavor,
I yearned for that bitter sweet.

A rarity of a commodity to young me,
that taste was a luxury

like a silk smoothie gliding
emerald delight over my tastebuds.

At a gathering, chance unveiled
the tub full of green richness.

A monsoon of memories flooded
memories back atop my tongue.

I scooped a spoonful of that paste
onto my plate, into my mouth.

Tears rolled down my cheeks,
a white flash froze my brain, I hollered.

And I discovered
wasabi.

The Kids of the Wat Thai Temple, pt. I

Waiting, we waded in the backlot with water balloons / aimed.
Secondly, we equipped Super Soakers to apply quick / hits
sprayed on butts; hoses were the hottest weaponry.
Skin drenched despite clothes queued to protect our bits.
Shivering, we waddled to dry off for the next game.

Allured by back scratchers duct-taped together with a net
to catch swimming shells with stickers repping
99 cents merch.
Cracked eggs, won prizes; coughed dough, conned
by a game for kids who didn't know a dollar's worth
but only valued the game as a carnival would.

Gut noises replace whining sounds with taste of succulents.
No stalling toward food stalls. Marketed towards mouths,
those half coconuts had us tongue twisted. Chicken meat
on sticks meet our belly, chunks stuck on teeth,
sweet mango and sticky rice parade our senses.

Flavored inputs to ears, wooden boards struck by mallets
we'd sigh low from, spotting dancers' fancy forms on stages.
Strung styrofoam letters carved with the paint of hued rages
hung like our heads dipped in sights and sounds for all ages.
We were ill-disciplined for our spirits, fulfilled our palettes.

Marching the second floor of balcony to catch Z's, instead
we dropped bees, believing we were Gods among ants,
though, statues of golden lions laughing at us running amok
as we pushed past our playful prank stared down by Yaks.
Master architect + time = well-defined housing the divine.

A grand structure roofed by a golden boat shingled red.
Guardians beside staircase before entrance was a trance
of surrounding aromatic smoke smeared with good luck.
Our faces open wide with eyes, we gawk
in non-spirituality testing our peace of mind.

We pray to take us back to the good old days
despite warnings from dangers of wistful yearnings.
But Hell, I'd give a 4.5-star review for this one stay.

The Kids of the Wat Thai Temple, pt. II

Raced up staircase escorted by green giants guarding entry
granted, let refuged on red carpets shagged, soft-lining floor.
We lined up in arrays before the golden statue of Buddha.
A nose-picking with presumed discipline, we sat through
back pinchings per improper postures in prayer pose.

Shocked, currents coursing, repeated sounds of resistance
followed by sounds of silence as we stabbed sticks
of burning incense on the body of The Great Jar of Rice.
Say chants to celestials, pray for what's to come.
Back down the staircase onto dining food hall, supposedly.

Lining elders holding pairs of scissors to give us our bald
from head to shoulder. Young men's rite of passage
when we watered off the hairs on our bodies.
In the bareness was a Holiness, cleansed and repented,
transitioned to an apprenticeship to monks for worship.

Orange clothes, two pieces, top, bottom, folds to mold
around ourselves, in light attire to hide our tiny penises.
Work meant we arose when black skies blurred blue
to sweep temple grounds with S-tier broom equipment.
We pray to skip to play and eat, but we pray and repeat.

We spent time, nightmares beneath the temple basement.
Dark corridors to us after seeing The Grudge with lament.
The crafty kid punkin', lead Ju-On a ghastly trip, lights out
preying on the weaker; bamboo mats to shield our bodies
from tile grounds but not the demon troller in the corner.

Hormonal raging in our bones, hurling male rising egos.
Porn to watch, dick pics to scatter, minds dented.
Pillow fights, pantsing bottoms, wrestling on floors.
That'll happen when you leave alone teenagers
in two weeks reserved for worship and prayer.

And all the Buddhist training, our parents thought
we were learning to be a fine example.
But I only remembered,
we were just kids having fun at the Wat Thai Temple.

I Have a Hard Time Putting My Head
UNDERWATER

Reminiscence smelled like chlorine.
Filtered membrane cleansed, it seems,
but this recollection came
from a shallow dream...

Goggles off, I saw
clearly, no one near me.
My being drifted to
the deep depth of pool.

I pooled my bets that I could float,
but I was ungrounded with oxygen fleeing.

This body of water replaced this body of mine.
Time was fleeting, and I needed to move.

The waving ledge separated life from death.
Stung eyes paled in contrast to skin's peel.

Ambient blue around
ears gurgled in diminuendo.
I tip-toed on concrete,
my muscles creaked.

The hand of God was me
to lift off from the deep end.
I depended on my own will
to not have wrote my own will
at so 'lil an age thinking these thoughts.

I zombie-walked my hands to reach
for the finish line. Fingers of mine
gripped with strength of mind
when I felt solid substance,

I gave out
one
last
breath.

Ma, I called, her

relaxed smile to neighbor
fades to horror.

Now, I have a hard time
putting my head underwater.

What's in a Name?

They called mine an alien entity
still foreign to this country.

Every teacher assigned me
a different name to fit
their designated tongues

the way American names easily do.

My full name
felt like
a fool's name.

How do you say your name?
I was ashamed.
Hated that my name didn't roll
off the mouths of monolinguals.

My name
slaughtered by uncultured thoughts.
My name
slobbered over in coffee shops.

And the kids fought me
because they didn't know
what to call me, backs
to the wall, fists raised
because I was raised

with my genes stained
from a generation of fighters
warring on the playground.

And they fought me
because my face
was different from theirs.
My eyes slandered with slurs.

My knuckles spoke more volume than my mouth,

for how else could they hear me
when I only knew how to talk
with my fists?

And they fought me
because my voice
couldn't speak up
for itself.

Four Elementaries

I. Chatsworth Park Elementary, Chatsworth

Kindergarten was a distant memory,
like digging through a basement's cavity.
I vaguely recall being stoned there,
burrowed in the corner like a loner

with soiled garments, dirtied
from a child still learning
how to use his words.

II. Kittridge Street Elementary, Van Nuys

Grades one to three,
but I was far beyond my 1 2 3's.
Bored by curriculums,
waves of thoughts kept me numb.

Teachers' snarks bursting imagination,
popped bubbles of my thoughts
that drowned out lessons
permeating through my skull
faster than the rest.

Counseling to console my stormy / tendencies
soothed by speech therapy,
rewarded with sweeties.

Learning how to use my mouth
instead of my fists
could only do so much
to quell my violence.

III. Canterbury Avenue Elementary, Arleta

I was most volatile
during 4th-grade explosions,
erupting the torment
of my confinement.

Like heels on hot coal,
my name was burnt,
replaced with synonyms
for more pronounceable Spanish / slurs
rising from my flame.

They faced me head-on.
Skin not black nor brown like theirs,
but tanned from ancestors'
hardships / underneath
the sun to blame.

Afterschool sent L.A.'s BEST
to pick me off.
3-to-1 to take on the outcast,
but I still outlasted when I blasted
their faces in.

The warden's office was my second home.
It didn't matter who started fights,
but who ended it.
and who drew more blood.

IV. Vena Avenue Elementary, Arleta

How did I wind up here, I wondered?
Do kids often drift
from school to school?

By 5th grade, I didn't understand why
the person who sat next to me
changed faces as often
as the beds I slept on.

My mouth dry from decibels screeching
for others to keep their distance.

But it seemed best I concealed my existence,
trailing the path of least resistance.

Through elementaries, I graduated believing
best to keep my head down,
like the whimpering winds,
imbued with silence.

Fight Club

Silent Voice

Why are you quiet?
We want to know how've you been.
How come you don't talk?

> *Why do you mumble?*
> *We can't hear you. Speak up!*
> *You got a voice, so use it.*
> *We're not trying to ignore you.*

Oh, sorry, this is your story, go ahead.
We didn't mean to interrupt you.

> *Wait, hold on.*
> *You're saying too much.*
> *You're talking too loud.*
> *People can hear you.*
> *You're being rude.*

What do you mean we're too noisy?
Is this too many questions for you?
Maybe if you told us,
we'd leave you alone.

> *Oh, you're talking to yourself?*
> *Keep your noise to yourself then.*
> *We don't need to hear your thoughts.*

So, you don't want to talk?
Why are just you standing there?
Can't think of anything to say?
You're boring.

> *So, we're boring you?*
> *You want us to stop talking?*
> *Wow, you're so insensitive.*
> *If you don't want to be here, then leave.*

You talk weird.
Are you high?
What's wrong with you?

Are you even listening?
You don't even look like you care.

Just ask, if you don't understand.

Stop asking so many questions,
how do you not get it yet?

Why don't you just tell us what you want?
Why don't you answer us?
Why don't you talk to us?
Why are you silent?

Hmm, he's so quiet.
I wonder why
he doesn't talk?

About Family

How do I talk about family
when I only talk to my family
through seasonal paragraphed summative text
messages composed through the internet.

I make my shots count,
hollow points do most damage;
bullet points to fix my silences like a bandage.
But, it's hard to put into words when
there weren't a lot of words exchanged.

My grandparents who flocked to L.A. chasing
the "American Dream" / in a cramped household
to bear three daughters,
the eldest bearing three sons.

Between two brothers, sandwiched
between knuckles, fighting was our common tongue,
when civility amongst siblings
were tested by the testosterone
innate in our genes

We swapped hands with treaties abstained.
Disturbing grandfather's calms, palms
relaying the power of previous generations, pain
upon our rears remembered for time to come.

When we broke / his slumber,
he went for anyone / louder.
Never weary, and only /
heightened in power
equipped with a broom,
                        sandal,
                                belt,
                                    whip,
                                        vine
where showing emotion was a crime.

On these memory shards I looked back / on
repressed memories becoming more clear,
it's no wonder my normality was illusory
with childhood mementos, I didn't hold dear.

Parental Guidance Suggested

I used to look up to Pa.
I remembered a "chill" guy
who'd only show us a stoic face.
Now, I remember his absence.

He gives us presents
in the form of car maintenance
so we don't resent him
for a missed adolescence.

Then, a kid couldn't see without financial literacy
the money siphoned from Ma's bank
so Pa could drink and gamble
and leave her credit score to tank.

Yet Ma had to be the center of attention
to have a bomb on the inside / activated
by a hair–trigger / with a more complicated
process to deactivate the explosion.

I suppose the apple flies far
from the wrath that chucks it.

So, I don't remember her as dearly
when she worked in the shadows
serving others instead,
waiting late nights gone to feed the light
where my grandma and aunts stood.

Now, I'm equipped
with a broken pencil on a blank canvas,
unable to sketch what I was drawing.

I told myself these truths I'd forgotten,
memories of the kid who would rage,
lost in his mind, rampant in reality.
His turmoil would turn to my resigned
indifference for my parents.

No, I Didn't Have it Hard

I was a gifted child
ahead of the curve
in math and science.
Too bored of standard schooling.
Didn't do well communicating,
shy and quiet, speaking silent.
But

no, I didn't have it hard.
I didn't choose to learn music.
Classical poetry bored me,
forcefully fed through my ears and eyes.
Now, I'm musically trained,
writing my stories, being artsy.
So

no, I didn't have it hard.
Being the middle child
between two guys
meant I wasn't a priority.
Followed rules
the elder one made
and the younger one slipped through.
You're not old enough, he lies,
but apathetic when the younger came of age.
Still

no, I didn't have it hard.
We had excellent conflict resolution.
We exchanged our words
with fists and bruises in motion.
We cooled off in our zones after pressure
and played video games afterwards.

Now, we're closer together.
So

no, I didn't have it hard.
I didn't have complaints
that I could voice.
My older brother and grandma
always knew best for me
with 60% accuracy.
My opinions didn't matter then.
So

no, I didn't have it hard.
I didn't choose what I ate,
There's starving kids in Africa,
they'd tell me to always clean my plate.
Now I'm not picky; I eat people's leftovers.
I have no meal preferences, no allergies.
I keep my body in shape.
Therefore

no, I didn't have it hard.
I wasn't physically abused
too bad.
Pa kept the drinking away from us.
Pa kept the gambling away from us.
It was mainly the yelling I didn't trust,
there were things to break
instead of us.

Sure,
it put Ma into financial ruin,
led to her spending being irrational,

unable to deal with being responsible,
but it enabled me to be financially stable
and self–sufficient,
paid my dues
being emotionally silent.

They're remorseful now
trying how they know best to repent.

Yes, I told myself,
I didn't have it hard.

The 1st Duodecennial

Through the garnet lens, I observe my past distantly.
At 24, I look back at 12 reminisced in memory.
There stood a kid fueled with rage and anger.

Before I was dropping bars, he was dropping bodies.
Before I was throwing hands, he was throwing fists,
throwing fits, bits of red in his stare.

A means to quell imbalance in his brain playing violins,
but stringent was he, forced art cannot sate violence,
marooned in his mind of torment.

For all I saw in crimson shades,
his parents knew only / a grim son's blades
with daggered eyes, my neurons stained with lament.

Through the telescoping lens, I see this kid,
opportunity to turn back time,
or give him admonition to alter his ways,

I wouldn't do it.

In the fire he had in his heart and heels,
he had to feel the heat.
For in ashes can we be reborn.

Across the distance of time between him and me,
foreign he'd be, but he was me, and we are one.
There's still that kid within me; I'm only grown.

To heal is to forgive the younger self I once was.
Every choice he made that I'd look down upon
has brought me up to the person I am today.

STEP II: WITHERING

I am a nerd.
Choked on words, diving deep into an imaginative mind.
Molded by science and tech, engineered prototypes.
Following the order of coding in my programming.
A gamer into the brand age and old, timeless.

"The leaves need to be dried and prepped for processing."

Flash! Player

playing games
Armored in New Grounds
was a ground-breaking Revolution
to Dance, Dance,
keep it moving,
keep me losing
to Kongregate at Ninja Kiwi.

Miniclip the no clips
of Street fighting and Tekken
taking me back to where I lacked
Boxed heads in an Age of War
taking The Last Stand
with Stick Man Sam.

Adventure Quests was a Dragged on Fable
like WoW, LoL, Mmor PG content plox.
Cool Math Games were The Halos
of my youth that zipped
and Sonic through
to point and click old memories
solving puzzles where I was

maRooned, eScape
from my world to
a Maple Story, as
flashes of screens upon late nights
filled my head with dreams

on consoles to console my departure from life,
where I can immerse into video games
and escape from reality.

Blind Sided

There's a stigma with astigmatism
by vision-unimpaired kids
of the Pacoima, 818 region,
who poke fun at the blinder
with words like "four-eyes"
before I'd retort with

but we're wiser.
And they shrug off
with daft minds, shoulders,
and their Budweisers.

The way brutes
bullied geeks
with words like "nerds"
to project their insecurity
with imbecilic stupidity,

Ha! I bet you're too smart for me,
they reply subconsciously.
When their poor grades degrade
their mental stability,
when their intelligence
needed compensation from the thrusting
of fists.

I made sure mine was faster,
living up to my label
and my wits.
Playground jocks joked
beating around what they couldn't understand
pitted against a mind with calculated plans.

I broke many of my frames,
glasses replaced frequently.
A threat to see their slowness clearly,
I was never good at eye contact.
I always waited until they contacted me.
Perfect-eyeballed folks think I can't see
except I saw   right   through   them.

The Strategist

There's nature within you,
and nurture surrounding you.
We've our roots, but barks
grow with the folks around you.

Chris,

I saw you.
Squat by you
before our 9th grade English class.
Don't know why I chose you,
but meeting you
shot up my trajectory
for the modality of my mentality.

No one challenged me,
made me think more critically
with your hypotheticalities.

Right or wrong was imaginary,
with morality making hairs turn gray
with your insanities.

My thoughts processed thoroughly,
you sharpened the procedure
excelling my functionalities.

Humbleness undisguised in your thoughtfulness
blessed with my dis-knowledge
of the rich background you left out
to remove my presumption for a book's cover.

Riddles and puzzles to solve
strengthened my resolve.
With elitist thinking,
my thoughts succumbed to superiority.
Board games and escape rooms,
logic imbued in strategy.

You went away, flew across the country
but laid the foundation
for my insecurities,
my complexities,
my base program
lining my comprehension.

Board Games

and why we play.

For settlers who took passes after classes,
schooling is pain, so break the mundane
to hang with nerds and play little games.

In a Tiny Town where we laid
Root-breaking Citadels, we gathered
through a Mystic Vale in Dead of Winter
with Codenames to Coup against the system.

World traveler Sushi Go eat on breaks
discussing Terraforming Mar-ginalized
groups beyond Happy Pigs and Splendor
believin' we're more than just basement dwellers.

We're resilient Chameleons with Resistance
to standard social norms, the true Nemesis.
These gems have undergone Evolution,
popularizing for accessibility beyond all dorms.

Engine-building is no work replacement.
These Cards aren't Against Humanity
as play should not be a Monopoly
but shared amongst company.

It's a Farsight to Kemet to, y'all,
as I share this Pandemic
for it is a Small World, after all.

Painted on a blank Canvas,
it is my speech therapy,
effectiveness in my words
when it comes to gameplay and strategy.

And that's why I play.
So, let's play!

A Letter From Prusa

Building its world from the ground up is all I do.
With gears spinning,
plastic churning
through my processor,

I make my master content with my contents
as I turn a string of nothing
into my inventor's mind
filled with endless everything.

From thought to paper, model to maker,
I print by design whatever
you've got baked in there.
Lying on this heated bed,
I procreate a newborn figure.

But whatever you imagine putting there
is up to you to figure.

Your pal,
Prusa

Remote Controls & TV

Molded personality from TV.
I watched, atop a bare mattress,
to sit and control remotely
the blank screen lit up / by
empty dreams screaming
with volume,
          stories,
                    make-believe. Friends who tell

about Adventure Times,
stray away from Regular Shows
about The Office, Madmen, mad beliefs
that we sit, we dull, we chill so lazy.

I'm Burnt, Noticed my brains fried,
                              eyes dried,
button mashing joysticks of the stick
that Scrubs our eyes, our heads. Our
Gray Anatomy is so grey
in our autonomy to blankly stare
so dully at our Community.

A dull be overthinking, but a Big Bang Theory
for these mind games is insane sanity
that Psych you out in the end.
Though, I know that you know
we try Breaking Bad habits
of leaving these screens on,
wasting electricity and our energy.

LED lights that blink / away our sleep schedule.
With circadian cycles needing more power,
ranging from Transformers
to transform the Gravity
Falling off our body,
escaping imaginative worlds of fantasy.

We play this blame Game off our Thrones
to not be defeated by the electronic mechanism
of this remote control that controls us—
by the media changing the medium,
we taste with our receptors.

It'll be our demise,
so change the channel,
step off the remote,
and take control.

Brickhead

I am Brick
Everybody like Brick
Brick is building block
Brick bother nobody

Brick make no problem
People don't hate brick
for breaking window
Hate use Brick to hurt people

Brick don't want to hurt people
Brick do nothing wrong
Brick thinks
people tell Brick what to do

Brick simple
Brick follow
Brick stay out of people way
Brick stay still

No fear
No sensitive
No drama
No problem

Brick don't feel
Brick don't need feelings
people can ignore Brick
Be like Brick

Poker Face

I didn't have an instruction manual to talk to girls,
but playing cards with you was hands down
the highlight of high school's downtime.

I was a fool housing
a deuce for a head.
Luck opposing my side
despite being seventeen.

Didn't have to be twenty-one
to drink thoughts of you
where I was gambling stakes
with no fancy suit.
No sharp diamonds,
just playing the right words
to play with you.

I tried to be cool,
but I was straight flushed out,
flustered by your presence.
I played the *Durak*
when I gave you my card,
I thought you'd deck me,
Egyptian Slap me, but
you saw that my ace in the hole
was having no BS in my hands.

I didn't mean to stare
when you passed *Spoons*,
you raised my pocket rockets.
You strung my heart
with your poker face
to get me like nobody.

I didn't call
when I had your number.
Red-faced as I
folded under pressure.
Couldn't bluff out
that I was the Joker.

Machine Learning

Engineering stemmed a great mind,
but its sentiments for my speech impediments
led me to only gander at the other gender
with weak words only leaving me to wonder,

how do I talk to her?

My words couldn't pass my filter.
Stuck in static, my brain's gutted
like solids working in a blender,
tinkering with how to approach her.

Bipolar moments conflict my confidence
to move past the initial inertia.
The shear stress twists my emotions
from a rigid model to angular motions.

Her hook slaughtered my chances
pulling at my elastic limit of success
where being ok is a constant factor
leaving me complacent to stiffness.

My mechanical mind to move was my intention,
but my disability to speak up had me in tension.
Braving confrontment has my intent shunned
by shutting down, feeling like an intense one.

It's a stress how much I strain
putting force over the area of my throat
from critical points I try to make
telling her what I wanted to say

how I feel about her.

On minutes standing by, I die behind
each moment of inarticulate text.
Getting close like a simp toting
dotted lines, but never making her mine.

Need software updates stat
to get my speech pattern unvexed
so this machine can learn

and I get better over time.

Serial.println("Crush #1");

```
#include <Aspie.h>
#include <Introverted.h>
#include <Highschool.h>

long courage = 0;
int time = 0;
String words;
float noise;
boolean femaleFriend;

void setup()    {
        Serial.begin(01012015);
delay(9999)
        pinMode(words, OUTPUT);
pinMode(noise, INPUT);
activate EmbeddingsFromLanguageModels
}

void loop() {
        while (LED = on) {
                if (femaleFriend == true) {
                        delay(10000);
                        courage = courage++;
                        time = time++;
                }
        }
        if (courage == 17) {
                Conversation(courage, time);
        }
        for (time <= 21; words == true; noise++) {
                analogWrite(progress);
                delay(10)
        }
}

void (Conversation) {
tone(oof);
Chai = noTone;
return Chai;
}
```

// Basic-ly, I thought
// We'd be a, compatible but my
// Visuals basic, can't see essences so
// Hard-ly we'd know, to fix it
// Swift-ly, but
// Let's GO, have a
// Jab at, script-ed it seems
// Rasp, very pint-sized to
// Bite on, but I've tried since we
// Met, lab-yrinths we R led through

// An addiction being rewritten.
// Restarting but delaying on dates.
// Deciphering your code is a troublesome road.
// The venom you injected to my systems made me numb.
// The bug you gave infected with malware made me dumb,
// you see? Plus, I excelled with glasses now to see sharp-ly.

// The past hurt like crashed computation to remember lines wrong.
// Neural networks cannot follow through the lyrics to your song.
// I simp-ly followed a program, one I was commanded to run.
// I'm conflicted on combating functions with bars you fed me none.

// You gave me a computer, despite instructions needing a rebooter.
// I wasn't programmed to feel unhurt, wasn't rewired to flirt.
// My hardware's all upgraded with software still outdated.

// You inserted your line.
// I ran error: 404 not found,
// which malfunctioned mine.
// I wasn't ready, so I'll shut d-

Countdown

My grandma calls me handsome.

I guess that makes "two people" a twosome.

I never had a threesome,

but for some reason...

I spent five years and evolved since,

But I've yet to have six.

I was only seventeen when I had my first crush.

Sure, I was a late bloomer.

I was waiting for that someone to be mine.

I didn't pay attention because I couldn't afford it.

I spent so long counting / down the days
'til I meet that one / when I should've been
counting up all the battles I've won.

My mind has infinite growth potential,
but They took up too much space.

I lived with Those roommates /
compartmentalized in my head,
but They know no boundaries.

They roam, but I've only ever been binary.

My thoughts are ones and zeros.
One side, too open, too honest, too blunt.
The other, too closed, too quiet, too sharp.
I've always been too little, too much,
But I've only ever been one body,
feeling like a nobody.

I'm wondering how I could be two
when binary numbers only go up to one.
Being two means I'm a ten in binary,
but I'm still feeling like a zero.

If only probability gave me / uncertainty
to be between zero and one.
People are a spectrum,
yet I've only ever existed
at both ends,
          outliers in a normal distribution,
                    integers among decimals.

If I cut myself
up in/to fractions to fit
               in this range,
I'd fall out / of the bell curve I tried
so hard to fall within.

Maybe, I'll survive
               before
               I'd be
               too
               undone.

STEP III: BRUISING

I am an adventurer.
An explorer of this planet, traveler of its lands
searching the abandoned and crossing places I've never been.
A novelty seeking skills through the madness in this world.
A solemn calm through cheap thrills and escapades.

"The leaves are beaten down, rolled, crushed,
and twisted to break down its cell walls."

Rock Hard

Sweat
      dripping
           off
               skin
                  on
                     hard
                        body...

You rope me in
with twisting hips
rubbing off one another,
fine jugs I firmly grasp.

You arch your back with
a rigid crack I slip my meat in;
fists, twists, sticks my feel in,
upright and erect.
Dived deep in that cleavage
tight with forearms.

With a curvature to caress
these slopes, I flashed you.
You're a mountain to mount,
a hill to climb.
I'd need trimmed fingernails
to finger that hole.

Your figure ate mine but not before
a tradition to believe another round
I'd need to dip and lather my hands
in that slicky, white substance.

To care, I've been there.
To harness raw power,
that's dy-no-mite.
I'm getting bolder.
And when I've reached climax...
I crash onto pad.

I do love
rock climbing.

Nature's Lessons

I cast my voice into the wind,
carried off to nowhere.

The mountains didn't reply.

I was waiting,
        practicing, but

Nature taught me patience.

I took it without reason.
I gave without receiving.

A living being taught me to accept that
        I don't need to respond, but listen.

                And all I'd need to reply
            is with a thank you.
        So, thank you
for listening.

Why I Hike

- NATURE
- ADVENTURE
- DANGER
- MURDER–

            ing my calves

as I cave in climbing up
mountain summits, I'm aroused
by Her curves. I drink from coconuts
that bust, my thighs'
ache as my pain dies.

I've licked sap off a tree,
I've tasted nuts fallen to ground.
I've sucked flowers pollinated by bees.
I've salivated over Mother's sound.

These treks brought peace
with silences that ceased
by critters' symphonies
and florae's prosperity.

Filling my soul with trust quick,
filling my soles with dust I kick.
We emerged from stardust
to exist with night and day

walking on this natural dirt path
artificially carved by ancestors before us,
guided by Nature
to show us the way.

To the Foos

and the road trips we venture.

It ain't about the ride but the riders
as we filled up our seven-seater
with memories and equipment
on roads alongside pitched tents.

oh, on trips to National Parks we go,

with jokes to Josh You Up
that'll make you Sigh On,
wanting More, so Have A
dessert pun on the rocks

among Kings' Kin. Young folks drive crazy
having near misses and pullovers
with sweaty pits swerving, but
Yo, Send Me That bottled thirst
from that Grand Can, Yum it be
on hot days to Stay, Cool, Ya?

To Yell Or Stone the ground with marching feet,
these mountains like Grand Teats On the land
parked alongside the road like a Deaf Valet
standing in A row, Heading like a sour batch

waiting on snapshots off screens
with all of us in, who shan't be pining
for forever greens to not be left
on Read, Wouldn't that be lovely?

Capturing moments with us frozen, all ready
with cameras to mark where we've toured.
So, park your tripod, and let's go already!
We got much more left unexplored.

Home on this Planet

The shortest distance between two points is a line,
the optimum length for my body where I lie.
Nobody, no other, no bother, so simple
for me to move in a pickle.

One story, one house, one garage, from which I gather
minimal belongings to fit in my pockets. No matter
too dirty, too rash, too cold, too hot,
none I don't mind leaving behind.

I wonder what you'd call home
for me, myself, and my bare backbone.
Give me two trees, two poles, two sticks, two rocks,
and I can make myself home lying in my hammock.

Leave No Trace

A squared one is just one.
The root of square one is still one.
So back to square one was going nowhere at all.
A scared one will have them come.
But divided by one,
multiply by one,
and you're still one.
Only when you take one away
will you be left with none.
Retracing your steps leads you nowhere,
and the only way up is to add another,
so make sure you leave no one behind.

A Nap in the Park

Yeah, I'd take a nap in the park.
No bed more comforting
than blades of grass
filtered through strands of hair.

No ridged backline of my leg
600 tinier ones wouldn't cross through.

No sound my ears wouldn't receive,
one to open air, other to ground.
I'm grounded currently,
feeling the roots support upon
the back of nape as I sod off to slumber.

Ain't no phobia but trypophilic
of sunspots on skin allowed through
by leaves leaving room for rays in.
No sunburn 'cuz Asian don't raisin.

Earth in her home I've been raised in.
Fields of dirt my mind to graze in,
I'm layin' 'cuz I'm lazy, so
yeah, I'd take a nap in the park.

The Winds

First wind, the howling tempest to surge me forward.
Second wind, the gentle breeze to knock me down.
Third wind, the roaring monsoon to move me onward to the
Fourth wind, the caressing whisper to slam me to the ground.

Fifth, sixth, seventh, eighth more to
torment me in unconventional convection.
Cyclic loading of the gale that sings in vivacious Spring
brings calamity before the banshee's screams.

Consistent, sporadic, incalculable, and chaotic to
determine laminar flows of whistling streaks,
not knowing how far I'll go...

Turmoil, invigorating, surging fury of
the storm's turbulence to lift me
without my heel's consent.

It's incomprehensible to be
backed by Aeolus's temper,
so come at me,
with that angered zephyr.

Free Fallin'

I recall my most relaxed experience
was one where the air cradled me in suspense.
Falling wasn't free, but it was worth the fee
to feel a minute turn from infinity to clarity.

Inside the cavity of the winged vessel,
anticipation tensing up the muscles,
pulsating through wind's circulation
as the bird's valve bursts open.

Through the gateway to sky oceans
landing with Tom Petty motions
off the arms of a mechanical body
spurting me out of its cavity.

10,000 feet above the ground,
naked airs slip, my ears sound.
120 miles per hour, my body falls
60 beats per minute, my EKG scrawls.

Soul reading at P(ea)Q R(e)ST.
Critical points of curve at lowest stress
where my body braved at the ready
with the whisked blows beating steady.

Strain release from my back drops
the nylon rainbow shoots, pops
my ears became a flat line
coming home, safely off cloud nine.

From the last I remembered peace
in my heart with tremors that ceased,
I fell through Nature's breath to dive
as she reminded me that I am still alive.

Coming Home, Safety

I remembered hearing "safety in numbers."
Congregated lots made me numb, heard
too much noise, chattering as crows did.

Safety is when I can turn my defense off,
where I don't need to keep my alerts on.
Crowds put me on the fence to going out,
but it's the natural outings I'm allured in.

Freedoms of folks are given much latitude
with different definitions of a nasty attitude.
Plenty of fellas may provide much gratitude.
However, still, I'd rather prefer my solitude.

Perhaps, my safety is unlike any other.
My safe is the type that's outnumbered.
In the dead of night, cold of winter,
alone on dirt roads do I feel unbothered.

The thrill of the outdoors provides kinder dangers.
No others but creepy crawlies so unwilling to murder.
Safety surrounds me where wilderness grows further.
Only the dark unknown to feed me sweeter hurt there.

STEP IV: OXIDIZING

I am torn,

    so

        lost, cold,

            and

                alone.

"When the walls are broken down, a reaction occurs.
Timing is essential to determine the fate of the tea's outcome."

LEAVE

The forks bear
but hurried it withers
These crossroads bring
but none or one,

Each moment
decided
A struggle
splits further

Action and inaction are
but actions
Inaction is easy,
The struggle

In all intense tensions
and divides
where the duality
must duel

for

BEHIND

paths bountiful
for me to choose.
decisions full,
 with the rest, I lose.

 a negotiation
 between logic or emotion.
 on every step
 with each hesitation.

  both actions
   are road maps of consequences.
   a singular river flow.
   for which way goes, diverges.

   that grew
    my mind in two
    of my voices
     to decide how I move

    words.

Cold Feat

How are you not cold?

I'm 1/16th Canadian, I joke
where the chill has given me
the heat, I'm stoked.

I'm part-yeti,
less time to ready
myself for the outdoors.

I'm allergic to jackets.
I just hack it with lacking
heat. I run in the rain with raw skin.

I take off my shirt,
give only the wetness
permission to touch me
without my consent.

I dive into shallow
waters of oceans
to embrace,
the only one blessed
to suffocate me in.

I wanted what was lacking to me,
where hugs were exotic entities,
and only the cold to give me.

It hurt me, loved me,
bathed me, cleaned me,
for the cold had been
my only source of warmth.

A Stroll in the Park

Yeah, I could die in a park.
Despite being in the dark,
I'm used to being unseen.

Besides murderers who wished to kill,
I've no life to offer.

Besides thieves who wished to steal,
I've got none of mine of value.

Feels like I'm comfortable
with the cold when it's all I'm in for.

With slurred steps, I've four in,
And already ready to turn in, so
yeah, I'd take a stroll in the park.

L.A. Freeways

Born-and-raised, but L.A. is a foreign jungle
as a prestigious destination
to those unrooted from previous generations
for ways to go on concrete roads.

City of weeping angels, where on-time is unlordly.
Where these concrete lanes are measured
not by distance but by time,

Why is the declared time the wrong time?

Because the shortest route is one
where people can cut me off
to cut me out of being included.

I'm lost in a sea of dates, exhaustion,
missed appointments, and flaky schedules.

Being part of the fashionably late
is a faction I wouldn't partake in.
Where people would rather look pretty than timely
because attractive people command higher authority.

It's a struggle already meeting folks
limited in grasping punctuality,
unease in a traverse from the 110 to Downtown
with walls unshielding me from gray noises.

These roads are graveyards
of broken dreams and morning meetings.
It's a commute to commit
breaking the illusion masked with smog.

This cityscape infrastructure is the antonym of time.
Trapped in metal and grime
to get from A to B
stuck in traffic, suffocated
by the air we breathe
where the only way to survive
is to drive.

Sunset Highway

A smiling face as I drive down the highway,
I squint, but I think of good ways to die today.
And there's nothing else left but to say goodbye.

I'll be looking for the happily ever ending,
but that sun is falling down,
and I don't believe in fairy tales.

Like a blaze of glory, blinding light,
I'll drive because it's what I love to do,
even if it's the last deed I'll do.

I ain't hoping for a passenger
to ride with me no more.
Ain't nobody else going down with me.

I hoped to live without regret.
A way to go, driving towards the sunset,
though I've never even met you yet.

A Letter From Camille

There'll be a time when I break down, but
I'll leave my engine running for now.
I'll keep exhausting until I burn out.

I've come a long way
and carried three of your generations.
I've been kicked, I've been hit, and I've been broken.
There was a time when it was hard to start,
hard to go, but it'll be hard for me to die.

I've locked you out when you tried to let me in.
Seen the smiles that you've always hated to show.
Traveled the miles when no one else would tour,
where no one else would go.

Heard your first scream, your first tears,
emotions you thought you didn't have.
I've seen your face no one else has seen.

I will be here for you when you're alone.
I will be there for the fight against the red tape.
I will be near your heart when your heart's not in it.
I have my imperfections, but I'm there until the end.

Your friend,
Camille

Drowning

Walls deafening,
sound waves crash like barricades
pushed back into traps of spikes that
pierce my drums.

Heats of bodies expand me out,
crabs chatter in raves
that bite my throat; I open,
but my voice won't come.

Volumes turned up, but
my dials buttoned down.
Epicenter of white noise,
foam percolates; I see level.

With each tides' crash, there's dissonance,
and I can't hear anymore
with the added distance.

It's strange looking at the crowd before me
and not understanding this language
I share with them.

I'd close my eyes, focus, and filter my resistance
to hold my breath, and each noise heard
has a world on their own.

Each interconnecting source speaks to none alone.
Closed surround sound ceases to exist,
the aching stops,

momentarily,

now points towards each realm's backbone.

My hearing is bipolar,
frozen thoughts I couldn't bear.

Sensory overloads when I lose my tongue
like a fish lost at sea away from home.
I attempt escape, but I'm caught,
        reeled in,
           sunken
           down.

I drown through noises undersea,
away from surface tension's volume.
Distorted voices fade away,
and my thoughts are sucked into a vacuum.

Ghosting

It's not rejection I fear anymore
when acceptance is just attainable.

With every bloody sacrifice, I cut myself
for each message I send out,
each time I try to reach out.

With every reply, I can heal, sutures on my wounds.
Everything I say leads me in the wrong direction.
It's all steps towards the luxury of rejection.

It's good to know I get a part of me back
when I get the feedback
for what I've done wrong,
what I could do better next time.

So, that's not what kills me.
It's dealing with apparitions,
ones I thought weren't imaginary.

It's when I write my lines in blood,
thrown to the void,
and I don't get those back.

I'm teased with a text only to be
left standing outside
staring through windows
because I don't fit in.

With each message drawn,
I'm gashed with scars,
but when I'm disappeared on,
I'm left bleeding out.

Defective Unbelonging

I wish I could shed tears to show my insides.
I wish I could be cut proper to fit into normality.
I wish I could cure my speech to talk properly.

It's a puzzle I can't solve.
This strategy to connect with people
is like 4D chess,
and I'm a pawn
who can only move backwards.

Shying away from this game
muffles my ears
when I don't hear
unspoken societal rules
I can't adhere.
How could have I figured
on what to do or say

when there's no formula I can follow
to understand how to approach people.

Made me wonder
why's it on me,

how liars gave me "gullible,"

a negative term that I'm so trusting
where I give people my face at value

when they don't value my opinion.

The same words can come from different mouths,
yet it only comes out creepy if you're ugly.

I'm a law-abiding citizen,
but these laws of attraction
made an exception
for me to be exempt
from interaction.

I've rearranged my limbs,
broke my parts,
but I've torn so much,
I'm a puzzle piece
nowhere to belong.

I look at people to understand
how they interact with another, flawlessly.
I try to imitate the way they move their mouths,
the way they smile at each other,
hold each other, share with each other,
but even with our shared language,
mine was still alien.

When everyone spits about love,
it's like L.A.'s got this inside joke,
and I'm not invited.

I don't know what I'm not doing right.
I tell myself to remain strong,
but if my script's putting up a fight
then I'd rather be wrong.

I'm told don't do that, don't say this;
if I can't be me, then I shouldn't exist.

I'm muted without the disability.
I'm invisible without the superpower.
I'm nobody without somebody.
I'm gone

without ever
having
left.

call of the void
(trigger warning: suicidal ideation/self-harm)

its easy...

tap the wheel;
drive off the road.

touch the rails;
power is shocking.

grab the lathe;
shred my hands.

the cactus is inviting;
give it a big hug
im so lacking.

turn the razor 90 degrees;
it's not first degree murder

if im killing the voice
inside my head
telling me how to end
my dread
when

i cant shed tears,
only shed faith.

i cant express sorrow,
only train to show despair.

i cant even show it
on my wrists
or my face.

no one to see
the wounds on my heart
until that heart is ripped out
splattered on the pavement.

where scars can flock people to share,
mine are internal.

where a wet face can swoon people to care,
mine is a desert

void of life

avoiding life

avoiding

you

avoiding
every moment my choice
to cease existing,
resisting the urge,
fighting the need.

every object is danger,
a tool or a weapon
sharp or blunt
to attack as i defend

or rather a cure
to heal my ailment
of living.

through every moment i can end it all,
one second to erase infinities of seconds
with just a micro twitch
to give out.

in every millions of choices,
i have to keep deciding
not to give in.

Snow

I.

My first snow was a sight to behold.
Capable body fierce against the cold,
carefree, living free, and having fun.

Climbing *Mt. Baldy's* falls,
sliding butts on chill hills,
Spewing balls like a Gatling gun.

A brother and a friend,
playing attack and defend.
Built a "snowman," underneath the sun.

II.

My second snow, we were cruising
down hills and having good feels
amongst angels and a snowflaker.

Unboring when boarding hurt like hell,
On *Big Bear*'s slopes where feelings swelled.
Rising to occasions were great before we fell.

III.

My third snow was a celebration.
We were warriors, we were conquerors.
We were fiery, we were free.

Jackson Hole's aerial tramway
to cafe top of the world,
Irish cream for glory.

It'd been our first through flailing hail leaving us blind.
Buried beneath heaps of cotton with peace of mind.

The howling winds that shrunk our peckers
burnt our faces like red hot chili peppers.

The frost bit through unintentional unprepared
light jacket, T-shirt, and wild hearts reared.

And a token for our bravery, Nature rewards
with retreating blankets revealing the sun's warmth.

This was a commemoration of our achievements.
This was a victory that we survived the worst.

Or, so I thought…

IV.

In the fourth snow, I walked alone.
Through a hallway of strangers,
I thought it was my time to go.

Deserting rationality,
deserting all rations

on a one-way trip up the mountain.

Beaten, fallen off the trail.
Crunch of sluggish treads left

fervent from heels of tar,
carrying steps of a dying spirit.

Gravity saps my ascent
as I descend to despair.

The *Icehouse Saddle*
sits the graveyard
of my final battle

to stand on edge
and one more time
hear the guidance
from my consciences.

Mountain

you are unloved
you are worthless
you are worthless
you are worthless

you've long eroded
this is your peak
you don't belong
in a world undesigned for you
there's no other kind like you
just let go
and let go...

don't you dare listen
the other misguides you
just give up
get off that ledge
And take a step forward

's peak

you are loved
you are worthy
you are worthy
you are worth more

  you've a long road ahead
   this is one peak amongst many
    you long to belong
     but you're uniquely designed
      there's still many kind to you
       just hold on
        just hang on...

        don't you dare listen
         the other misguides you
          don't you dare give in
           get off of that ledge
            and take that step forward

STEP V: FIXING

And I took that step forward...

"Oxidation is stopped, leaves are heated."

The Step Forward

Where are you now, voices?
Silent, awaiting eyes
I can't see.

No one told me to go up
there on stage,
but me

at my first open mic.

Did I do it for the girl
who pushed me forward?
Or was it for me
to get in my word?

Silly I must be,
beneath the spotlight,
with ukulele in hand,
a waning in my voice,
a weakened mind
waking

to bare my soul
and confess my feelings to the girl
with a song made on the fly.

Words came easy.
Programmed with honesty,
but difficulty in each line,

I could die
coming in with nothing
but a heart choking my throat
like a child learning to speak.

I survived my lowest point upon the tallest peak.
So, how much harder could this be?

Perhaps, every rise comes after the fall.

It's a tragedy my apathy motivated me
for I'd have never gone up
that Sunday, jumped to my feet
if I cared what they were thinking.

They only see bravery.

Dare I call it courage,
for it be discaring disposition
when I stepped forward
and gave it my nothing

and it was worth it.

To jly

A grand voice from a galactic mermaid...
A radiant smile stunning me for a while...
Blood rushed to every corner of my skin
when I saw your face.

With hair flowing like strips of space
fallen to the stars dipped in the cosmos,
with chords that vibrate in your singing,
so surely in my mind, it kept ringing.

But only in movies can a beauty fall for the beast,
imagination runs free without the fallbacks of reality.

You're here in a pretty place,
I'm standing there
awkward and displaced.
I'm graced / disgraced in your presence.
I've been bumbling and stumbling,
unsure of what to say
because how could the popular girl
fall for the ugly nerd.

But, I'm glad you didn't ghost me,
a chance to prove myself.
I understood we couldn't be more
than I initially thought we could.
I can't change the parts that made me
who I am,

so thank you

for seeing past first impressions and accepting me.
You're the butterfly's wingbeat that typhooned me,
the first stab at my armored heart.

Be it worth to make your smile,
at least it'll keep me here for a while
                                    l o n g e r.

To Soul Stuf

When you witnessed innocence in my voice,
vulnerability at my first mic,
you saw a promising future,
a place in a community I'd like.

You read my soul where I was illiterate,
sneaking past my faulty translator,
smuggled back the words to my mind.

You found my value where I was blind.
You spewed ember flames,
entertained my strains
with smooth jazz oozing from your brain.

I showed you my skill
with a technical mouth
sporting an engineering folder.

You showed me my will
power I didn't know I had
potential I can be bolder.

Charged with the catalyst
zapping the creator within me,
you whipped the chain to spark my engine
starting the motor revving thanks to your ignition.

A speedy voice, quick witticism,
with haze that seeped
through the cracks of my armor.

I'd dare not tamper
with the cogs of destiny
to risk not having met you
and finding my artistic identity.

To Ariel

Deep, dark blue, cerulean so surreal
unbeknownst to wide-eyed me.
Lost in darkness, but colors fade
to brighter blue when I saw you, funny man.

You pulled my hand, and we swayed
to worlds far beyond my comprehension.
You brought the cheer to be near
when I was wrapped in tension.

Like Sylvia Plath's horse,
you rock that mane, my main man.
You assumed your dread
locked you out, peaked your cool,
but your hair don't define you,
you were tight the whole way through.

You got the feet to keep us
running but not smelling sour.
Even defeated, you stayed
past midnight plus three hours.

You fly high so aerial, rising
amongst fakes because you are real.
City of smog, but the air I'd reel
is a natural cleanse to the feels.

You understood I didn't aim to inspire,
yet you stood over my shoulders
to shoot even higher.

You're a champion of my creative self-worth
when I tried to cower in camouflage.
You surrounded me with love to my artistic birth,
investing in me where most would dodge.

You'd give to make sure
I didn't suffer from bleeding out
giving me the final impact
to shed my armor free.

To Arianna "Lady" Basco

When I first met you in 2020,
I thought
I was looking at a 20.
I know my vision ain't perfect.

Because 40?

Still looking gold AF.
Still looking spicier than Tabasco.
Still looking... out
for the brothers, the sisters, and the children.

Lady B, when you lay these beats,
everyone's hearts beat.
Every one... becomes a ten in their arts.

Boss 'cuz you're Bosco.
Team B sides... deserve an A+.

Besides,
being Filipino,
filling that pinoir, feeding the people,
herding free thinkers and brave souls,
putting the soles back in our shoes
when our walkers have been broken.

There's a magic in your words
that puts a magnet to our worlds,
whirls harder than the gravity
that brings us down to Earth.

Puh-raise the B when you raise that bar.
B-yootiful in the forms you teach.
B-yonce in the power of your voice,
B-yond but within reach.
B-cuz I'm always down to go downtown
to hear that sound of your preach.

Opening up the pages to Palms 23:1-3.
The Lady is my Shepherd.
She makes me stand up in gratitude.
She restores my soul.

So, cheers to

Reverend Lady Lord,
Arianna Basco,
First of Her Name,
Speaker of Words,
Opener of Spaces,
Gatherer of Beings,
Leader of Freemen and Brave Souls,
Khaleesi of the Academy of Upward Palms.

To Palms Up Academy

I lay these beats
tailored for a list of
all extraordinary people
who can go
afford to catch
rays of sunshine
on a hot July day
when we got paid then,

but I kicked myself on the curb because
I've missed camping;
I've missed parkour;
been lazing like a house cat
changing the channel
feeling malcontent
only aging with time
askin' how people have low highs?

When my mind gets fuzzy,
the sage in me tells me:
"Don't get mad easily.
You're a fighter
with gauntlets on
'cuz your soul's tough,
crying tears of joy
where you do you.

So, feel alive,
snag the lens of a camera.
Put some clothes on and dress up
like a magnum's bullet firing off
the ricochet, taking flight
like a Bluejay meeting

my key to drive
to the maximum
down Beverly Lane,
where the air's real.
Not the beach, too much sand there,
but to where people give high-fives
all around, feel the people in
the spaces I'd bet any chips."

And she's just sellin'
art there. She's chillin'
with no jealousy
by a fig tree, baby,
just enamored
with cherry cheeks
to get lost in.

And, she's magic, man,
her flow is just music
like Philharmonics
that puts the rest to shame
that has me marking my journal,
and share a look
with the guts to ask her:
"Yo, lean a little closer,
ok, please?"

With no convincing,
her words are like some lit
features of ash, leaving behind
burnt pieces of crisp wood
that can make a meal,
smelling of nutmeg and

freshly baked cookies
with apple ciders
that makes me go crazy
to roar eternally,
rise like a phoenix.

Even if Recess was finished
at the sip of my last yawn,
I thank all for inspiring me to stay cool, movin'
me forward to never lack puns,
'cuz we'll be robbin' the space
knowing home isn't a place
but a community,
ever-growing,
constantly building
at Palms Up Academy.

Step VI: Drying

I am a creator
collided imagination and reality
storytelling my experiences
           in humor,
                in beauty,
                        fusing views contrastively.
I am on the Path, guiding me through my creative ways.
I lacked mastery, skilled in discovery,
jacked in all trades, master of mine only.

"Tea leaves are dried and packaged, ready to be served."

Invest in Community

The rich will tell you
that they can take your money
and spend it better than you.

The rich will tell you
that all you do is squander your money
but they can invest it and multiply their own greed.
So, I'd say

invest in community.
If I put my money towards stocks,
I gamble my currency to support only me
and the make-believe lines that determine our GDP.
But why would I do that when I can

invest in community.
My money goes to real minds,
real support, real people,
real opportunity to get love from breathing organs
to get hugs from the people
who will fight with me, die with me,
dine with me.
When I feel a loss of faith, in hope, in chances,
I could fall back on a caring community.

When I invest in community,
it's a privilege to save money,
but it's an honor to save my people
from debt, from poverty,
give them freedom to exchange their chains with time.

Millions of dollars
have nothing
on tens of hearts.
There's more value
on a collective of creative minds
than mining collective bundles of cash.

It's a shame being poor is a crime.

But being that poor is a definition in this nation
measured by money
and not by the bonds we have with one another.
So my better currency goes
into the resource that matters most to me.

With pooled minds more potent
than numbers in bank accounts,
with more virtues of empathy and connection
over vices of greed and selfishness,
I can't see why we shouldn't be
investing in our communities.

L.A. Frees Ways

Freedom ain't free,

but if you can afford the struggling opportunity,
in L.A.,
we're always alive.

Living out every day
different from the day before.
World culture melting pot
in one store.

Stories plenty in diversity
across neighborhood arrays.

The range from beaches to mountains
echoes ample experiences.
Stay grounded reaching stars
sparking the ignition to traverse locations.

You can never run out of ways to entertain.
Gaze upon the sights,
gays up on the sites
gave up on being sold
as lesser
and being more
than what they are told.

The ostracized from other states
seeking sanctuary,
refugees
for being weird, being weebs,
being niched, being themselves.

Unrestrained to express identity
because you can be you
free in your ways,
here in L.A.

where the way to be alive
is drive.

This Forest Speaks

Lost in an enchanted wilderness,
layers of marked fibers pressed
with etchings to take my mind
to another life, another time.

These hands hover over figures
as I hear voices from its authors.
Memories stoned within barks
as I journey through their arcs.

Lit lanes by fireflies blanketed
night skies guiding targeted
soles to souls sheltered within
vitalized branches paper thin.

Home for the homeless,
a reclusion from stress,
this forest is a growing organism
to allure the curious to its chasm.

Sheltering poets and adventurers,
storytellers and creative warriors
who laid their immortality projects
upon leaves shelved by its architect.

These trees incorporated history,
where knowledge is a necessity
of essential oils who grazed their hands
designed to be shared on public lands.

Lost in space and returned to reality,
enlightened after leaving this library.
Another visit, my interests piqued
because these pages speak.

5th Wheel

The 5 of us in the car.

My older brother in the backseat
holding his girlfriend's hands,
my younger brother in the passenger
with his arms back
to hold his girlfriend's hands,
and me in the driver seat
holding the wheel

to get our fill of meat.

I drive us to K-town to get some beef
as I balance it out with my comedic relief.
I turn the radio low to play ambient romance
the way my brothers do with their partners.

I eat with no worry of a significant other
for my fries to eat and not share with another,
or be that guy to swallow all the leftovers.

It's good this way, for just us five
as six can't fit no car.
It's best to have back-up,
a car needs 4 tires,
and one to spare.

Roped in to watch other's hearts to steal,
our parts to carry ain't concealed.
I have the role for a good deal,
as I play 5th wheel.

L.A. D.R.E.A.M.

I swallowed my pride, but I'm still hungry.
Starved for attention, but I wait for the tea.

Breaking bread to break the fast
without breaking the bank being free
meeting dreamers to shine at last.

An infinite amount
of what to throw at me,
I always stay insatiated
to brew my artistry.

I made myself financially stable.
Figured that'd be sustainable
to an artist not slaving away
for an insentient corporate entity.

Seems like an impossible dream to make it.
My dreamers making it day by day
being broke in their bank accounts,
but

Debt Ruins Everything Around Me.
Blame it on the bankers
determining our worth with their money.

Numbers on an unsolvable score,
leaving them wanting more
from us,
leaving them lacking our trust.

They're only accounting for the rich
who have their yachts and fancy ships
not counting the true value

when we maintain our relationships
with ourselves,

to have lived a life, level up my experience,
as a sustainable artist.

I was born on a Sunday,
raised at recess,
life is such a beautiful mess
with what I came up to be.

A Tea Break

Hey, you.
Yeah, YOU!

Though, I wonder which voice you hear when you scan
these lines.
Is it your own, or mine, or a mutated version of both of
ours?
What would you hear in your head if you hadn't ever
heard my voice?
Yes, I'm going meta here and talking to you directly,
kinda.

I mean, not directly, but like,
I can see through these words the way your eyeballs
move. *wooohh*

I wonder what kind of reader you are. How do you read?
Here, for this bit, this is about how chaotic my speech is,
my authentic unedited(-ish) speech sounds like.
I'm a bit confusing at times, I'm kinda like this in real
life.
I've been told I talk too fast.
I'm working on that.

I use hella more fillers than filters.
I'm working on that, too.

But, um,
here's an intermission.
I just wanted to check in on you,
see how you're feeling.

You've been reading a while, huh?
Perhaps take a break.
If you're a marathon reader,
rest here,
or not,
don't let me tell you what to do,

but do take the time to reflect a bit.

It's dope enough you're even reading a book.
I wonder when we'd cease productions,
if books ever transcend the physical plane and only exist
digitally.
I suppose we'll cross that line when the time comes.

I offer this tea break before carrying on
because

you may feel uncomfortable,
you may feel challenged,
you may disagree,

but it's your right to your feelings,
and, in the end,
we're all human.

Flip page to continue.

STEP VII: BOILING WATER

I wish I could **focus**. I wish I could hear anything other than the voices in my head and the neighbors who blast **sound** with that deafening music because I can't feel my room. It's not even to be bothered by but **disrupted** by something I care so little about. Something not even in my room, but it's something all I can think of to **combat** the sound of the voice in my head. And when I faze out here now, it's empty, but the **silence** in my head is still screeching the white noise from my laptop. The screen showed **with** nothing but the fans whirling. Saturation has taken a deep nosedive, and there's **death**. Nothing else to highlight my **eyes** because all I've seen are dead. There's nowhere else to muster the energy to **brush** up much else. Why I try when it doesn't go away, how I've been trying to get **up**. I told myself I was. Where was the point of this? Where did I miss it? There's **nothing** much else going on, Where did I leave it? Where's the positivity in it all **but** vast emptiness? Unvalued words of mine. The only thing I managed to absorb was the TV **static** I get when we've decided to think no more. I wish I had something more beautiful to say. Ideas locked, only piss words flowing to the urinal in my hands.

My room is my **prison**.

Masking

I can't believe I'm becoming a social worker,
getting put into a job I'm unfit, underqualified for.
So what am I here doing this for?

I'm incapable, inadequate
to be doing a job that requires
much education
when I have a background
with so little information.

Whoever was in charge
of role call should be called out
for running a task so full of doubt.

My
      Social
           Skills
                Don't
                    Work.

I wonder how people who don't mask
complain about putting it up for a bit
when I've lived my whole life doing it
without having to ask.

With everything going online,
my face is unseen,
no longer on the line.

Eulogy for Sleep

I'm being drained by this bed
that does nothing but to exist.

My energy wears down
                    as I stay down.

My mind tells my body to rise
                    but my arms can't lift.

I'm so tired,
      and I haven't done anything yet.

I have things to do,
why can't I do them?

                        Damn this bed.

I once ran a marathon and again.
I climbed the equivalent of Mt. Everest.
But that body doesn't feel like mine anymore.
For here I lay, awaiting the next day
                        and the next.

Still Stuck

I am in bed.
I am not at rest.
I lie completely still.
I am still not at rest.

The screen flies past my fingers, and I feel tired.
I've done nothing, yet my rest has been sold
with a to-do list I am so unwilling to do.

I remember when I had life.
Straining,
      pulling,
            stretching my muscles,
               sweat off my skin
for I am at rest
when I am in motion.

Realized scarred, I melt with my warmth
sleeping with eyes open,
and I'm not recovering.
My energy sapped from doing nothing.

Soundless mind silences fast
to how much time has passed.
Let me go, claws of lethargy.
Get off my soul, blasted misery.

And it hits me,
I am not at rest but in so much hurt
with only thoughts to occupy an already
slain head of dirt.

Nightmares of Relentless Torment

I.
Working from home is a prison.

I'm constrained to a black-cushioned padded chair
with my laptop on my lap as thousands of pixels light
up my face, still-beating heart, and four-walled cell.
The doorway behind me served only as a gateway to the
kitchen and bathroom, sustaining my body with food
and excretion, a closed cycle in this confinement system.
A single square window is but for my eyes to escape.
Yet, what purpose does this window serve when I'm
only awake when the sun isn't?

My ears are filled with keyboard clacking, mouse-
clicking, and fan whirring. The fan couldn't keep up
with the heat generated by the computer, which was not
enough to shield the chill's grasp on my bare feet.

My vision waters down with my eyes wearing off from
staring at the computer screen of sheet-metal models
and LED light fixtures. My eyelids weigh a ton each.
At my last glimpse, before I enter another darkness,
I witness my CAD-modeling program blip an error
message:

"RUN. RUN. RUN. RUN. RUN. RUN."

My fingers slink from the keyboard. The cushions of
my chair conform around my legs and torso as they
inch their way up my eyes, swallowing me into another
realm.

II.

       This wasn't the peaceful falling I remember from skydiving. I'm in some space that's lacking stars. This dimension pulls at my internal organs and malleablizes my insides by gravity in every direction.

The source of this madness illuminates. I've seen a full moon but not one in full bloom, trickling turquoise and stealing my entire vision.

I gaze upon this indigo abyss, this chrysalis orb, expanding to cover up the bulk of what my sights can see. With edges rimmed with hairy, golden flakes like redlines on an insomniac's eye, the astronomical entity shines brighter and brighter, blinds my eyes, and shatters my vision.

III.

       I grip hard, with my entire front positioned flat upon the sandstone dome that sheds dust on my clothing. I tense my muscles to ensure I don't fall off the dome–like structure that might be the head of a giant statue. The statue's form grazes against my exposed knees and elbows. I strain my forearms to proceed to the top.

I'm inside a giant tomb. Walls on either side of me were unreachable, separated by a bottomless chasm below. The lantern on my back illuminates a ten–meter radius around me. Despite this, the hallways beyond only show endless darkness.

There's no sound but my limbs shuffling alongside the giant's head and the strained breathing of my airflow. There's no other smell, but one of the ancient times I taste from the surface I climb.

With primitive eyes, it took my heart to detect the feeling that something exists in the darkness beyond, watching me, judging me...

waiting...

With a grunt of pressure, I push myself up to the top of the dome. I stand firm for just a brief moment until the stability of my grounding submits to disintegration, melting into an oozing puddle of muck.

IV.
      The hands rise from the sludge. Several arms reach to grab and pull me down. Layers of skin with food, grease, and oil bloat its body and drip onto mine, yet I recognize its face. Its disfigured form was one of gluttony and agony.

It was one I see every time I have to stare at my reflections on glass panes.

I hated looking at it. I hated it with all my blood scratching underneath my chalkboard-like skin. I clenched my fist and my teeth, as I poured a flurry of fists onto that image.

My roar tears my throat as I turn the mush beyond its
original dysmorphic figure. The screams were a mixture,
as were the blood that came from me and the creature.
I dived deeper and deeper into the body, fell inside the
dome, and merged into oblivion, suffocating my voice.

V.
        I open my eyes to see darkness again, with a
blaring spotlight over me. Four gavel strikes upon a
sounding block seep into my ears. I turn around and see
the bench with wrinkles upon a judgmental face.

"You are guilty." The judge condescends in his judicial
gown. "What have you to say for yourself?"

I scoff. "I've nothing to say to you. Your justice system
is broken, unfit to judge me, taking a blind eye to money
that feeds you to stay blind."

I turn around to be stopped by another in a black robe
and hypocritical eyes.

"Then, confess your sins to me." The priest declares. "I
will forgive you when you tell me all you have done."

I sneer. "Who are you to call yourself righteous when
your crimes stretch further than mine. Spitting about
love and God when all you do is spread your contagion."
I spite this creature and turn around again.

I stop dead in my tracks.

"Then, tell me. Why do you fear to speak? To feel? To love?"

The vile creature mimicked my movement as I stared into the mirror. I don't recognize the being before me. It was hideous; it was despicable.
I'm consumed, again, by anguish and torment. My head, aching for me to stop looking at myself. But I can't seem to turn away anymore.

"I hate myself.

I hate all that I am.

What is there to love about me when no one else does. With what body of mine, no matter the stats composing it, can be found lovable?

How do I rid this feeling of longing for any kind of affection but not lose the remaining value I have for myself?

I'm so lonely.

I hate that I am programmed with weak power in my voice of integrity, which only leads to the opportunity for me to be abused, used, and taken advantage of by those around me."

The figure in the mirror frowns. Its movements no longer match my own as it raises a fist to break through

the glass, shattering it into thousands of shards that cut
and blind me.

VI.

I'm in bed again.

Did I burn another day
or lose another night?

The clock in front of me shows 6:66PM in the evening,
but the light from the window above my head shows a
darker shade than night. I see my room in a strange blue
filter.

In my peripherals, I see a TV beneath the clock. Above it
is a ragged bunny doll, dirtied from being bullied in the
mud. I try to move my body, but it's not in my control.

I see the door, open ajar, to the right of my peripherals.
A pair of little eyes peers at me. The little child steals a
moment of my stare before closing the door completely,
leaving me locked in with the bunny. The bunny doll's
eyes light up red, and its mouth cannot move, yet I hear:

"You are unable. You are unable. You are unable-."

It rattles its head, and I feel thousands of voltages
crackling through my body as if being Tasered by an
unknown entity. I tighten my gut, squirm, and try to
break free of my body before I pass out. I-

VII.
Wake up.

I lay in bed,

still waking,

still dreaming,

still..

My computer screen whirs.
Nothing stirs.

I can stay in my nightmares,
for these are bliss compared
to the plague roaming beyond my walls.

Hell is brewing,
Between my mind
and the outside world,
the struggle is real.
The problems are real.

There's no other purpose for me here.

I've been awake for a whole year.
I swore off drinking for a whole year.

Quarantine 2020,
and it's time to migrate off this coffin
that I've made for my slumber.

Time
to go outside
and take my mask off.

I opened the door
and braced for impact.

Life in Death

I have cheated
Death so many times.

I've asked Them out to dance
but They didn't even want to Tango with me.
I thought if I learned the Cha Cha or the Salsa,
They'd be impressed,
but I'm still here,
and They keep
rejecting my invitations.

Many times They allured me
at the wrong place, wrong time,
I'm alive
by misfortune.

But Death found me
                unlovable
to welcome me into Their home.

Yes, I cheated Death,
but Death cheated me
when Death took out folks who didn't deserve it,
and left behind people who do.

Now, I'm stuck on the streets with misery,
toxicity, people who'd treat me
no better than you did.

I think I'll take Life instead,
and show Them
a better time.

STEP VIII: DAIRY

I am armed with a pen
        fired from my weary crown
                to lay it down
        about a world
        that makes no sense.

"Make sure you lac those intolerant."

Conjunction of

Love is
pronounced
easy
with others

I must be
of my own volition

accepting
people
and I see

understand
I must
be

these
are

my Hemispheres

Evil
backwards
is to live
comfortably

objective
in this world

the masks
wear
off

why
speak up for
cause

voices
mine

Wet Guys

Beautiful body, he said to me in the locker room.
Thanks, I replied when I dropped my robe.
Helped me prepare for my first time
                                    at a spa.

Eight inches longer than theirs,
the hair on mine more present
than the elders' heads bare.

No glasses, hair down,
stumbled across signs.
I gotta shower first.
Barely saw shapes,
but I witnessed some thirst
when I caught their gaze.

I'm reminded by older, white men:

Magnificent figure.
I used to look like you.

Their reminiscence of youth they had
helped my self-image,
appreciation for my body,
with the courage to dive in.

Though, I wonder what stops envy hands
from seizing strangers' thighs.
It's tougher to be more aggressive
to a youthful male, fitter in size.

I wonder what it'd be like
to walk down the street
every minute
        of every day
to be called and complimented
by every guy I don't know
        on every corner.

I won't ever know, as a guy,
to worry for the next comment
        turn to threat
        turn to horror.

I'm privileged to feel safe wherever I go.

At the spa, they can only gander.
Even if social rules bend there,
they can't attack my consent
shielded by my gender.

I get it when women are oversaturated,
                        full from compliments,
while the average guy is starved of any sentiments.

It's remarkable how many remarks lays a mark
on a person's comfortability with comments
unsolicited, regardless of good intentions or not.
We won't know the fine line
when I took a little comment to get me confident.

Fragile masculinity stems from a place of insecurity.

But, we can't brush off what a woman has to say
for how often do we brush off a woman's voice
when a man brushes off a woman's choice
by brushing it off with having a bad day.

We can turn to the double-edged sword
of reactive justice from his or her word
or we take proactive measures teaching them young
on engagement behaviors and how to be better ones.

To a topic, I've only dipped my toes in,
I won't ever fully understand
what it means to be a woman
who can't live freely
until we rid this world
of toxic masculinity
and redefine what it means
to be a real man.

Gatekeepers / Floodlights

You see them speak, and you tighten up.
They squirm their faces, disgust with distrust.
You hear them on teleprompters
telling prompt, there's deceit amongst us.

You know the ones
who feed you anger
that crawls beneath your skin
when you scroll through screens
with messages from boomer kins
and unkindly Karens

who are
uncaring to people's struggles
that's purely theoretical to them.
They confuse privileges with benefits,
overlook disadvantages to others.

They feed off your anger,
supplement their mouths
so their eyes can stay blind
to prejudices that don't apply

to them, our existence is abstract to bigots.
They'll pull the trigger
transferred to machine-gun bullets
of words loaded with nuisance.

They'll plow you into their traffic,
cut you off before you can think.
They'll blind you with high beams,
blare their horns before you can think.

They're troublesome, uninvited residents to ears,
like roommates who don't pay for rent.
They squat without paying dues
as their fumes have you choking on your words.

You blink away the channels,
but their volumes hold magnitudes.
Earthquake and shatter your struggle
as they set a match to gaslight you.

They don't care that they're wrong.

They'll take your trauma,
stamp their invalidation,
send you on your way,
to fall on their slippery slopes,
striking you with straws
in their constant fallacies
of falsely statements
supposing "factualities"

when in reality,
they're too proud of their insecurity,
projected, from being excluded
as victims of an oppressed society.

So, they gatekeep your history,
locked out of sights
as they drown you out
behind their floodlights.

Compartmentalization

We buy shelves and cabinets,
definitions to promote organizations,
categorizing our items into proper containers.

How neat it is to put objects with similar descriptions,
put them in their place, where they belong,
easier to find where they go.

Separate clothing by place on the body,
differentiate foods by types in drawers for our fridges.
Space for sauces serve no purpose than
to serve its main dish, supplement with flavors,
but useless once the meal's dished out.

Labels on boxes can only generalize their contents
until you reach inside and find out
everyone stores items differently.

It's easier to know where to look
when you have all related materials
in a box labeled as you do,

and isn't that neat?

And how about people?
How easy it is to classify suicidal folks,
the neurodivergent, the weirdos and the freaks,
the disabled, the poor,
the undesirables,
and leave them at that?

How easy it is to lump hate onto a group,
give an entire spectrum only one definition.

When you attach a label to a person,
you put them in a box,
group these folks and treat them all the same,

where the labeled are based
on their usefulness to society,
their sacrifice to corporate greed.

The mute don't have a voice,
the deaf can be drowned out.
We aid those who can't see in HD.
There's no OCD on human categories.

Our pigmented skin had the same roots,
so we generalize ourselves into the masses
boiling down all we are, all we've experienced,
put them down in a compact,
3-dimensional box
squashed down
into a flat piece
of cardboard
on the streets
to have others
see us
like all
we are,

and isn't that neat?

Imaginary Lines

I am Asian-American.
At least, that's what I put in the box
so the government can identify me,
categorize me in prejudices,

giving us imaginary lives

that others can judge as a model minority.
Their kind ain't kind to us,
the ones who'll lie to us,
tell us we're not like them 'cuz we're Asian.
Our eyes like slants they slur,
cursed they don't trust,
but they can't see
in our culture / the real gem.

They tell us to stand by like a bystander.
But I can't stand on sidelines no longer
when they tear this place up asunder.

They told us to stay down, do as we're told.
They called us yellow to keep us mellow,
but they're too colorblind to see the gold
melted in our skin.

In school, they taught us the ABCs,
and later, about our DNAs
defining us
by previous generations generating nations

telling imaginary lies

that my genes say
I'm 70% chinese, 25% Thai,
but I'm tired my identity is based
on these nations telling me
I ain't 100% human.

How can ethnic identity base on science,
when mine was rooted in my culture?

On the geography we're born,
determined by our ancestors
who came and boarded
these lands of nations
divided by us.

By these artificial constructs,
we carry our genealogy,
our intergenerational trauma of category
telling our neat compartment of identity.

But who can tell us who we are
from the ordinances of nationalities
when they're drawing

imaginary lines.

Bloodsuckers

Mosquitos suck.
They drain our life force,
little by little,
leaving bumps on our skin
from drinking our reds.

The silent assassin at night
with my body a buffet
unlimited to feast
with my limited sights
to swat a bank shot
at that discreet buzzing

left in dread. We keep slaying,
but they've more, gauging
on the richest veins on our body

with needles to transmit diseases.
They come in billions,
been around for billions.
Their life spans over ours,
We spawn, we die
but they're generations' generations
forever sucking our
    Blood.

      Bank

        Tellers
        tells us
    to fight for the cause of capitalists
      as pawns to be sacrificed.
     Wishing for vagrants to cease
     with their blue brutes busting,
   redlining hazardous investments
    draining hoods where bodies lay
       on the streets.

Their lives spent
forever bugging us,
feast on our mortgages,
pouring the richest in vain
as they hoard billions,
stealing from billions.

Buffer from wealth classes,
hitting bars to getting buzzed,
celebrating with banks shooting
away broken dreams.

They sigh, lending as if
to steal our greens
by bumping off our kins.
Little by little,
they drain our livelihood.
Bankers suck.

Pigs on the Lawns

They're dressed as pigs in suits
during daylight, golf tees on
downtime most of the time,
basking in the poor folks' blight.

For the hoarders who maintain
the status quo of not fighting
for the class warfare fight,

these words are for
you who privatized areas,
replaced squares of green on our maps
with tainted, egocentric debauchery
of mockery upon these lands of scenery.

Your country clubs suck;
they've ruined this country.
Detachment of reality
through environmental degradation.

Give back the greens you stole from this nation.

Nature's parcels divvied, filling
with a darker shade of green
in the wrong direction.

The ones on yachts
ought to dismantle
the land they've "bought"
back into the public's mantle.
Turn back to public parks
stolen from dollar sharks.

Millions are stolen from millions
to support individual real estate
reeling state's contributions.

The squandered water reserved
for your lawns reek of privilege
for pouring filthy dollars wasted
upon this land you ravaged.

On these lawns, we scrawl,
this animal farm under war,
even pigs are more valuable,
at least they feed the poor.

Dear "God"

How dare You.

How are only some of us
born into Your conformity
and the marginalized are
labeled as a deformity?

And what about Your hypocrisy
promoted by brainwashed dynasties
who ruled with outdated hierarchies
using Your commandments,
Your extreme beliefs to delete
outlying "abnormalities?"

Now, Your preachers praise words
they can't even follow,
comforting the masses with weightless blankets,
no warmth, just guidance that's hollow.

You're an opposition to evolution.
We can grow to become better, but
you stay in place, keep us tethered
to obsolete ideals, anti-progression.

Your miracles are shortcomings
with our health blessed
by doctors and medicine.

With Your mysticism dried out
by streams of scientific revelations,
You'll only be left as a remnant
for lost souls, faith for the broken.

And this blasphemy
ain't the last of me
to spew against Your
designed catastrophe.

How typical for a man to steal a woman's work,
I attribute our world's beauty to Nature.
I give You no other credit.
For this world would thrive better
without You in it.

All* Lives Matter

It's hard
to disagree
with that statement
when you can't hear
the asterisk attached to All*.

It's ingrained in the slave masters' memories
for followers who preach (all)
written within parentheses
to not include the lives of their enemies
despite the teachings of the Christianities,
but I guess that's the Evangelicals' hypocrisies
to spew All Lives Matter followed by ellipses...

It makes sense.
You ask a kid, and they'll agree
because it's easier to read that
rather than the terms and conditions that apply
that no one can read to its entirety.

And ain't nobody got time for that.
White supremacists can't
understand anything abstract.
You pray to their God it's all an act.
Matter of fact, it's why all lies matter.

Shame they co-opted pro-life to promote pro-lies.
That's their life to be vouching for the un-alives
despite their lives not on the lines
forgetting there's lives at stake and lives on stakes.

Throughout history was a history,

erasure of those who don't fall into conformity.
The Devil's lefties executed,
conflagration with witches in flames,.
ethnic cleansings,
        autists euthanized,
                and it was All those to blame.

And it never ends...
We hope, we pray, we fight,
we get slain again
            and again
                    and again.

But in the end...
            it still
                    doesn't
                            matter.

Down of a System

What happens when we put our money to God,
and He puts the money back into His pockets?

We praise bills, sacrificing bits of ourselves
trying to reach an unattainable dream
of being in that hedonistic state,
entering His domain, a demonic estate.

When we worship the paper,
we add a price tag to living.
We invest faith to the dollar, we
lose faith in ourselves. We

chase after numbers,
not realizing numbers go to infinity,
still incomparable to human life, priceless.
When we fall for the currency,
we get washed by the currents, see?

When taxing payers turn to prayers,
these pastors' CEO turns churches, incorporated.
These religious institutions don't pay their fare dues
when they're doing pyramids
off your free labor.

Profits to the prophets hinders progress,
producing false narratives of a God to
prey on the hopeless.

Giving your money to God was a distraction
to prevent action against polar opposition,
a red herring from the real rulers of this nation.

The idea of God was a means to control
you, believing you've more
in common with Him than
the bodies laying on the streets.

Our capital loses, only siphoned away
by preachers spewing nonsense
when we only making cents
compared to dollars by these parasites.
Manipulators spin tales of impropriety,
targeting the lost, devoid of certainty,

but it's the ones with the most to give,
the grandest souls to share,
and the wealthiest minds to know
that the people with the most dollars in their banks
got the least compassion in their hearts.

A Solarpunk Future

I grew up working in my field to sustain myself,
but what if we worked not out of necessity,
but of desire?

What if survival wasn't the goal
because we already mastered it?

What if the goal wasn't to accumulate
more than your neighbors
but to live the best life you can?

Our fundamentals of shelter, food, and water
became sustainable through green efforts.
Nature takes a reclamation of its land
as we took a reclamation of our play,

when we no longer competed but cooperated,
shared our resources pooled together.

A future where the current value of the work
we're giving isn't equivalent to us surviving
but to us thriving.

Education is imperative,
understanding how climate change
has accelerated in the wrong direction
by our efforts.

Urban planning should revolve
around people over economy
as Earth is an ecological system
before an economic system.

We no longer prioritize killing for commodities.
We take L's to make-believe GDPs
when it can be a means to lower poverty.

Lean manufacturing discusses types of waste,
but it doesn't talk about how every material
comes from the same atoms that make us.

When global conglomerates shut down
because we no longer give them our money,
but we show each other peace
over lack of profiteering off wars.

Globalism's responsibility
on global emissions are still reliant
on our consumerism and hedonism

where capitalists assign dollar items
to control our artificial constructs
by marketing off our insecurity and security.

How can free market work
off the chains of the enslaved,
criminalized the marginalized
when corporations make profits off prisons?

This is no war against individuals
but against the system
and the corrupt who uphold it.

A system where ninety-nine problems
give you ninety-nine more,
flawfully designed to pit the poorer against the poor.

In a nation much more divided than ever before,
we can't be on opposite sides but besides one another
because the only way forward…

is together

for the final frontier against inequality
is the fight against the greedy.

"Environmentalism without class struggle is just gardening."
~ Chico Mendes

World Peace Parade

We'll never be united until we stop
seeing each other as the other side.
The label slapped on boxes we assume its contents
except we're more than the boxes we are contested.

Everybody's concerned with being right
but forgetting those left behind.

Nothing with looking down at each other
when we should be looking forward
to help people get up from poverty.

The culture conflict is a distraction
with naysayers as catalysts for delayed resolutions
when people argue without logic but beliefs,
when people base their worldview limited by their senses.

The rabbit hole is far too narrow to go down
unless you have a limited scope of acceptability
to broaden your empathy.

Can't come out of hiding
when you weren't shoved in the shadows,
No pride without others shaming you for existing,
No movement without pushing back.

There's a polar opposition
against oneself for breathing freely.
That's why we fight for social justice.

Privilege is good,
The first step is acknowledgment
and how to wield that power to help others.

Ask not the what, or how, but why
these issues exist and dig deeper.

We can't be reactive
by investing in punishment and retribution
but empower proactive prediction and prevention
to understand the other side.

Free speech not hate speech, but I hate
that they slap the 'speech label' over their hate.
There's a freedom to impress with ignorance
but try expressing open-mindedness.

Some want to watch the world burn,
but many want to watch the world
flourish.

Where some have designed this world for a few,
we can redesign this world anew
to include everyone
one step at a time.

Although I am as qualified
as the next misinformed on the megaphone,
it's imperative to be open-minded,
challenge your ways of thinking,
and be willing to accept that your viewpoints
can be expanded and further developed.

This problem is far more complicated than I can
answer, yet what we wish to strive for
can be more attainable.
But I believe we have the resources and capability
to achieve this future.

STEP IX: SWEETENER

Take your time. Drink some tea...
don't forget to rest and breathe.

First Impressions

So, tell me about yourself.

Well,
I lived a lifetime before this moment,
                    and I've more to go after,

but I cannot contain my experiences
in one-hour sessions.

They seem to judge so well off one-hour interviews,
a quick summation of my skillset
packed in one sitting
of interrogations.

When I'm underqualified,
I oversimplify,
for when I show my worth
I become overqualified,
like my qualities don't fit
to what they're looking for.

I have to remind myself
when they move forward with another,
the direction of their velocity
isn't always right for me.

I am more than my paper.
I am more than the paper I make.
I am not a paper mache
packed into one body.
I am not a nobody.

My life, my experience,
needs infinity to sift through.

So, I won't dare
to let them make me
feel less than
who I am.

I won't dare
let them
define
my value.

I know my worth.

But do they know?

Alexithymia

I wish my mouth had the same smarts as my head.
My flapper runnin' slower than synapses gone ahead
with the IQ of my lips lagging behind
the thoughts in queue lining up my mind.

This language is English,
but the feeling is gibberish.
Words inhabit that name,
but my mind stops me
from saying something
I can't even define.

No attributes / but all the characteristics.
Simply put / it's complicated to relay it.

Mental blocks / bouldered pathways
rewiring terminals / loose and ending.
No comms, my computer / bargaining to stay on.

Lost signal, but my chips / driving me
defenseless. Loading screens / progress at null
to infinite / standstill from regress.

Spinning hourglass / wheel of doom / error
code messages / puts my mind unease / you
watching me deteriorate my face.

It's error to feel new-age tech / shutting down
from a simple trick / stoned still you
think / of me as I lose all latency.

For a term to torment how
indescribable to name it,
I'm ineffable to write a piece
of all the ways to describe it.

Dating Game

Play is a way I know how to say,
hey, I'd like to get to know you better.

I thought, as a gamer, I'd have game
because in-game, I can see
whether you're easygoing, competitive,
sore winner, sour loser, bitter or chipper.

I can see you on your edge,
I can see the way you think,
the things that make you tick,
the ways you make moves on me in play
is better than the moves we make in day.

But the words off your chest
are no more calculated
than the moves in chess.

This wordplay to maneuver to make you unbored
is more challenging than the play on words
to keep you onboard to keep playing
on this board game.

It's much easier
when the rules are written,
unlike the dating game
where every rule's unspoken.

And why's dating a game?
It's lame to play on emotions
where risks are high stakes
with stocks in motion.

When online is on-the-line
where bumbling my lines
set my chances burnt by tinder
to mingle with bagels is no harmony.

No way for me to get to know you
than to play with fire, playing like liars.
Many players won hearts with lies
and many more players too hard to die.

How do I play with you when we play
with our words behind our masks?
I'd rather play with masks off
in cards out of clubs
lacking diamonds to die on
and strings detached from hearts,
having extra lives to restart the level in-game.

There's only one heart to destroy in life.

Insane it is that
there ain't no tutorial,
there ain't no program,
there's not enough RAM to get me to run.

When I'm feeling displaced in this place
putting me on display for putting on
this play I made for every pair
of eyes I get lost in, I lose altogether.
But for every game I've lost, I get better.

And that's why I play.
So, let's play.

Stutter Speed

There's that feeling
when my mind travels past Mach 5
but I'm unable to let the air flow
through my pipes.

I was terrible at advanced physics
because I couldn't neglect air resistance.

The words can't pass the coefficient of static friction
multiplied by what I normally force equals tension
in my speech.

I'm impeded,
unable to get past the gatekeeper
called my yapper.

Stuck in turbulent
chaos to calculate
the speed I need
to enunciate.

I'm clawing at my
throatway choked
by the dirt that buried
my voice six feet under.
Stopped,
as I try to find the first word
to break my sound barrier.

Ms. Photographer

You captured the moments in the apertures,
you captured the momentum of me
falling down the stairs feeling no harder
than me falling down for your stares.

These broken bones hardly compare
to the broken spirit when I don't say
what I want to say
     to you.

Your glances lingered a little longer,
the covers of your eyes made me shutter.
The distance from your cap to mine, I'm taller–
           ating
to pass through my filters.

I see clear through lens
the warmth you gave made me stronger
to stay by the end of the day
that I couldn't have not shoot my shot.

I couldn't let you be another one who got away,
and I didn't want to miss my chance to say,

I see the magic you capture with your camera,
so I wanted to tell you about the magic I see
       behind the camera.

Snapshots, pt. I

I randomly accessed my memory,

and I

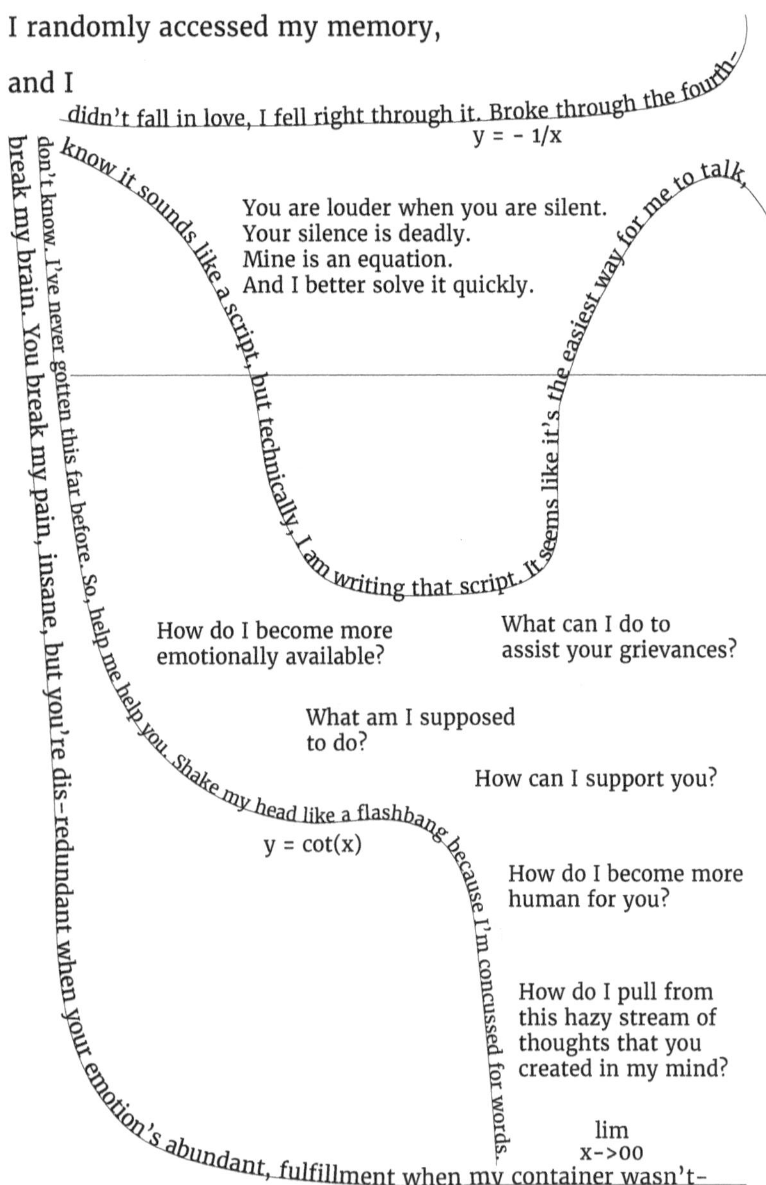

didn't fall in love, I fell right through it. Broke through the fourth-

$$y = -\,1/x$$

know it sounds like a script, but technically, I am writing that script.

It seems like it's the easiest way for me to talk,

don't know. I've never gotten this far before. So, help me help you.

break my brain. You break my pain, insane, but you're dis-redundant when your emotion's abundant, fulfillment when my container wasn't-

Shake my head like a flashbang because I'm concussed for words.

$$y = \cot(x)$$

You are louder when you are silent.
Your silence is deadly.
Mine is an equation.
And I better solve it quickly.

How do I become more
emotionally available?

What can I do to
assist your grievances?

What am I supposed
to do?

How can I support you?

How do I become more
human for you?

How do I pull from
this hazy stream of
thoughts that you
created in my mind?

$$\lim_{x \to \infty}$$

158

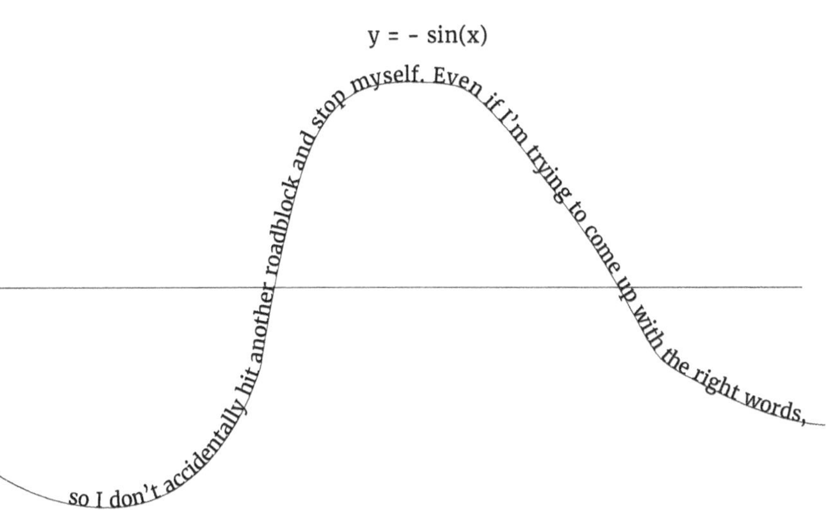

Understanding this mind is an understatement.

then maybe it's not about saying the right things. I suppose that is better than me trying to say something deep, insightful, and meaningful. Even though it sounds more robotic and mundane, I thank you for your patience with my silence shattered into a stringing flow of simple thoughts in my lined structure.

I know it might seem a tad bit more different but I have that effect of me stopping myself in my tracks, so this is what I have to do for now. Software updates to follow.

But you

fell

for me?

Well,

that has never happened before.

* End transmission*

Capturing the Moment

I used to scoff
at all those pieces
the poets and the songwriters wrote about.

I didn't get it
        until I caught a glimpse,
                a fraction of that feeling,
                        and I see now.

I felt it
when you had 4
of your fingers
laced with 4 of mine,

how lucky I gotta be
seeing you / wake up
4 different times.

Walking away always with that
                        derpy grin on my face,
following the moments after your embrace.

I hate that I
        can't explain
                why I love
                        what you're doing to me.

There's no logical reasoning behind it;
it's no one feeling but a system of explosions inside.

Your image is so invasive.
Your smiles kill me softly.
Thoughts of you turn my belly to jelly.
Your name drops make me all giggly.

It's a grand mood to be hit by a pick-up truck
going 120 on the freeway.

I see how this feeling inspires so many
people on this planet to write
about the same stuff repeatedly.

Even the meaninglessness in this life
was meaningful to me when you sat
in my car beside me.

You discomfitingly make me
feel comfortable in your presence.

How someone named light contain darkness,
but that doesn't make you any less
                              than who you can be.

For I'll be there when you're surviving,
        so I can be there when you're thriving,
                and I'll be grateful for this feeling to be
                undying.

And that's the beauty of being boundless
when you were off the restlessness.

I could write to infinity
        about that moment we laid endlessly.

Even when I bored you to sleep,
it bored into my mind
how deep I didn't mind
my mind was awake alone;
I dared not look at my phone
to shatter this

illusionary eternity looking at you.

And it didn't matter how long I lasted.

All I know
        without knowing the time
                        at that moment...
                was timeless.
Your smile: priceless.

In that stasis, I made this whole thesis I've written
that has me spittin' I'm still smitten by you.

You tell me to extrapolate off past data,
but you assumed you were just another point.
You tell me you don't want a temporary,
                but you're playing with an eternal.
You fell way past the regression line
                        and dropped the R-value.
Mathematicians will tell you that's a bar,
                        and I know you got value.
Now you got me believing I ain't dreaming no more.

For I see
the sea of words above your head,

so vast,
it would be forever to reel them in,
fish each one out to give to you,

but eternity's a time
I can spend
to go through all of them
with
you.

Still Shot

I am in bed with you.
I am at rest.
I lie completely still with you.
I am still at rest.

Your hair runs past my fingers, and I've entirely
nothing else I'd do but to rest my soul on you
with a to-do list I am so willing to do with you.

I remember I am alive.
Straining,
pulling,
stretching my muscles,
sweet on my skin,
and I am at rest
when I am in motion with you.

Red-lined scratched eyes melt from your warmth.
You sleep with your eyes closed.
Your body on mine to cover me
Our energy shared, I'm noting.

Sounds of mine sigh less fast
to how much time has passed.

So, let me on, claws of pleasury.
Get off on my soul, blessed company.

Nothing to hit me,
I am at rest with words you've heard
and only thoughts to occupy all ready,
layin' heads on dirt.

Snapshots, pt. II

My memory is randomly accessed.

Maybe

I can't sleep at night. You keep me up when your heart beats close.

You sleep so beautiful, but everyone still wants your eyes.

You're no ________, you know that / I know nothing.

How can I be so careless when my self-care seemed selfish?

My pen's the only that can sneak past my zipped lips. I'm speechless. You stole my words when I hear you breathe into me.

$y = \cos x$

Just because this is not easy doesn't mean it has to be difficult.

You hurt me as you unhurt me.

I've been taught to treat no kind my wrong choices seem to always come a bipolar choice: speak or not speak, and my

like me with kindness. I treat my friends more with generosity. How I treat my relationship with a piece

I can't manage my tasks. How can I manage uncertainty? I need to delete controlling alternatives.

$y = |x|$

I'm an honest person but not transparent. I'm blocked by my flow stoppers.

You make me shut down without the restart option.

every day is a battle against uncertain dis-confusion,

$$\sum_{i}^{n} x_i = x_1 + x_2 + \ldots + x_n$$

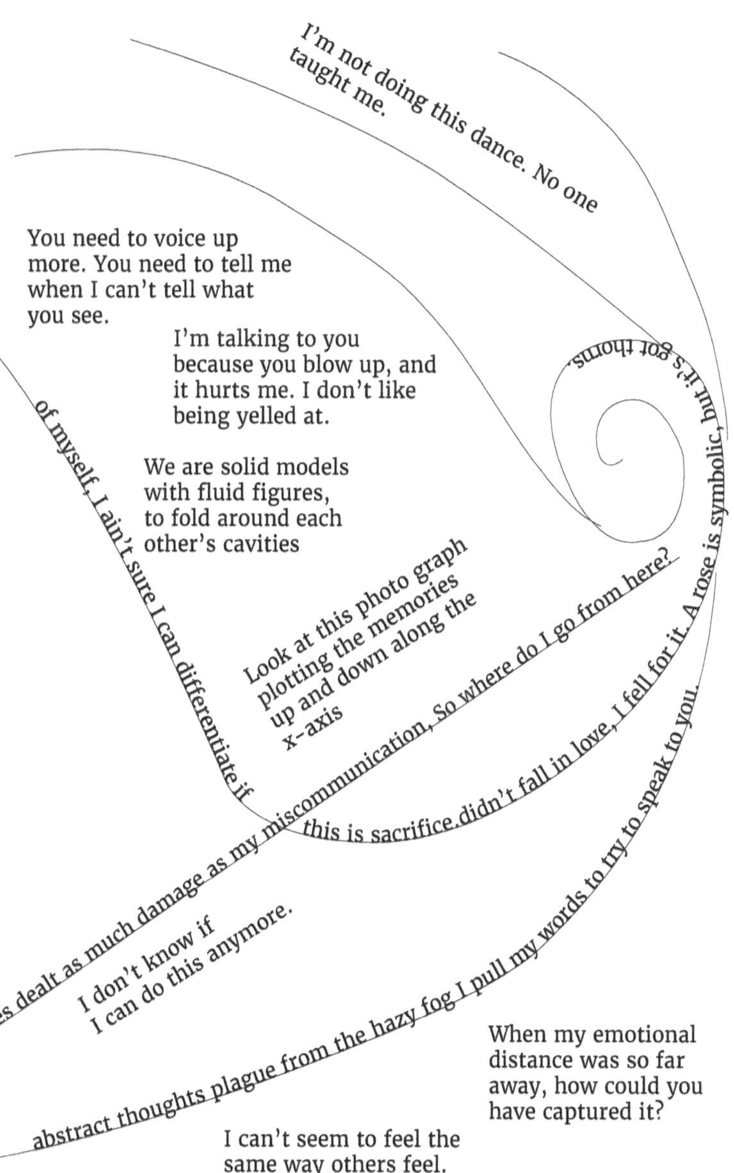

I'm not doing this dance. No one taught me.

You need to voice up
more. You need to tell me
when I can't tell what
you see.

I'm talking to you
because you blow up, and
it hurts me. I don't like
being yelled at.

We are solid models
with fluid figures,
to fold around each
other's cavities

but it's got thorns.

of myself, I ain't sure I can differentiate if

Look at this photo graph
plotting the memories
up and down along the
x-axis

So where do I go from here?

A rose is symbolic, but it's got thorns.

didn't fall in love, I fell for it.

ences dealt as much damage as my miscommunication,

this is sacrifice.

I don't know if
I can do this anymore.

my words to try to speak to you

abstract thoughts plague from the hazy fog I pull

When my emotional
distance was so far
away, how could you
have captured it?

I can't seem to feel the
same way others feel.

How you delete my words, I wouldn't understand, but
I will keep it in a backlog somewhere in my broken
storage, chaos cluttering my pages.

because I can't seem to say
I do l—
i do… liee-___
I do?
do i ______ u ?
i l l l L
i i i i i
iii lll

(i can't cant *cant* **cant CNAT** go in…)
(my words, cant cant cant cant cant cant Kant)

(why can't I say,
can I not because I don't mean it?
can I not because I can't define what it means?)

crazy in ______

can I —-

I luh- ____ oo

Huh?

170

what did you say?

you... _________ me?

you _____ me.

You.

____

Me.

Wow.

You never happened before.

Flash Freeze

Hey, she slides into my ear, *let's go outside*.
My butt off the bed creaks the mattress.
Slipping on a sweater, dressed;
door swings wide

to a whole new world, we go;
contrasted temperature
from warmth to cold
but the calm shared

in the fifth snow.

We taste cotton candy through our pores.
Pure flakes, one there lands on noses
with our tethered shackles in rhythm
finding each other in our steps,
following another's footprints.

As to not get lost in the fog,
we followed the trail laid before us
by wayfinding our trailing heartbeats.
The beaten track as we got beaten down
by rising hail's power, not enough to break us.

We broke down the fence
tumbling towards the pier.
We played defense
as the tempest went harder,
making us blinder.

We came upon the stage crashed by waves' reared.
The tides' of the lake stampede, braying bridge's
support structure, keeping us afloat.
We marched with all our strength
against fury blades of the storm.

There was no way the follower would have noticed
before pushing the one in front nearly off the edge
as we presented before the blankets of the abyss.
Only imagination to describe
what laid beyond the mist.

Spirits' warmed up
despite faces being number.

Adventure is calling,
Nature still has my number,

and I must answer.

Overexposure

I once lost control of my fists
when exposed to extreme pressure.
Now, as a pacifist,
I lose control of my words altogether.

I can't show the deconstruction of my mind
when multiple inputs to a closed system
gives no time for me to output from my mouth
the required flushed fluids to respond.

With no coolant clearing nuclear energy,
no command to circumvent
overheating streams,
who'll know when a pipe will burst to vent steam.

There are only so many measures
to avoid melting down.
I'm irritated, aggravated running
rapidly rushing recklessly
when I try to calm the inner me.

Glitches in comms, fried circuitry,
calculations running incorrectly.
Every noise, every flow,
hurts my own body.
No more control than before,
but directed regulation
using contrasted circulations
destroys my navigations.

I'm leaking from my brain,
I'm cooling off by spilling my beans,
but you're overwhelmed

when I overshare.
You're annoyed, I'm overloaded,
You break down, but mine is seismic.

Programmed to not hurt another,
all the damage redirected to myself,
shutting down when I'm jarred,
hardstuck, out of flow for words.

The Darkroom

Rumination
is a dangerous room
to be in hibernation / when I sleep
holding on/to your last message
like a Teddy bear
of thorns.

How could I have known
that I was raised under toxic masculinity
to bottle up my feelings,
keep it locked behind my mouth,
just for me to swallow my emotions,
still starve for attention,
and defecate it into the trash where it belongs?

When my voice overheats without the vent,
to breathe in your volume without my consent,
I'm stuck carrying your emotional baggage
leaving me behind to take emotional damage.

How could I have known
that noise would be my pain?
In a household loud all the time,
my treatment was silence.
My silent treatment became weaponized
so you couldn't understand how I'm feeling,
and I couldn't give you feedback
on the hurt you fed me back then.

How could I have known?
I'd grow up to be so quiet
that you couldn't understand
what I mean to say
when I say

goodbye world
when you
were my world
that I needed
to step off from.

Snapshots, pt. III

Nothing is truly random.
Even computers follow algorithms.

I felt–

My words
these
t
y
4
parabolic
fades

I wish you could C, when you tried to reprogram me, it bugged me,

when you couldn't understand my functions,
I didn't understand yours.

A rocky relationship. Fractured my words. Thoughts incoherency.

Ordered inconsistencies in my lines,

though my flaw
designed to you
is perfect for me

shake for color,
polaroids
his polaroia
our paranoids
paranoia
curvature of down–up

Your anticipation was of three periods instead of one, so how could I know what I could have done?

error 404: find you find me found

these emotions i don't understand

These snapshots of moments I captured you,
print thousands of thoughts you inspired,
kept away from you
behind my throat.

I can write to infinity / because of you / my mind is a bullet
at the speed of light / you shattered my heart into fragments,

and I see

all

all

It's still

I wish you can read into my muted speakers
that spoke louder than the barrages of questions   to create
trapped by my voice.

My silences have been open to interpretation
but I never meant for them to open your wounds.
When your experience was for treatment
mine stemmed from trauma.

I am the antonym of emotions, but I am not its antagonist.

I could be,
I am not,
at once.

a monologue,
            a monologue,
                    but it takes two
a dialogue between me and you.

This perpetual motion of fate,
No guiding voices
but mine to tell me
how to navigate this relationship

that needs to happen before
deciding difficult choices.

Shooting Stars

I broke

        my mind
                into constellations.

I'm burning out my oxygen
when I contemplate how to carry on
                        holding your hands.

On feelings I can't let go
when your celestial body transferred heat
                                to mine.

I stared deep
into those hazel eyes
                of the storm.
The universes behind them hold oceans
                                I drown in.

I swam in that moment of eternity
getting lost in the abyss of waves
                        healed by your light.

How do I free myself
of something so bright,
        to fall off the deep end
                        depends
                                on whether
                                        I could grasp...

when we were
        still shooting stars
                over long exposure
                        wishing to capture
                                these moments
                                        with you.

Each stroke of your hair
had me breast stroking
in your breathtaking
apertures.

When you looked like stars
                        still shined
                                after all this time,

how do I feel what I can't define
when I focus into your lens?
How do shades of pain fall
in the same spectrum as your love?

How have you made me speechless,
when you guided me towards the words on these pages?
I watched you
        hold your trauma,
                your stress,
                        when you could be
                                holding
                                        onto me.

To leave nights on sunny rays,
which story is canon to my destiny?
With no guiding stars to tell me

but me,
charging into the veiled fog of my future,

braving the uncertainty,
riding the edge of infinity
        with you
                forever
                        in eternity
                            or
                                    forever
                                    in memory.

Step X: Boba / Bubbles

South-East Asian-American
Unlimited potential
Triumphed champion
Infinite
Carving my name
Hard-earned effort
Always growing evermore, never tame
I am a drink by the name, a thirst quite the same

Two Funerals

I.
The noon was warm and blue,
green fields bloom from tears of dread.

His smile stitched neatly, eyelids at peace.
The box lid open for rain to pour in.

Stories shared about him were foreign
from elders expressing emotions
with bawling laughter
to drown out
weeping sorrow.

I hoped his face conjoined joy
concocted with the sadness
fallen from my grandmother's eyes
into her brother's casket.

II.
His photographs were a success story.
Lottery tickets framed his altar
of his passive passion from winning
all that Life could offer him
before passing him to Death.

We emptied our eyes, our glasses,
with 2 scoops of rice into our bellies,
memorializing the man who lived full
as his physical form be incinerated
leaving behind
bare bones.

III.
The next morning was cold and red
with grey puffs covering azul hues.

I don't remember
the last words
I gave my dad
nor him to me.

Then I saw his resting face.

I felt the atmosphere of the room
in my heart,

and there was nothing.

No liquor on the cheeks,
no jolly memory,
no sighs for relief.

He awoke from his slumber,
greeted me,
and we went to reception.

Like a standoff,
we ate our sandwiches,
waited for whoever would fire first.

He did
by noting the rest of the folks have arrived.
It was time to start.

My father spoke and brought life
to his mother
one last time.

IV.
She was buried in Rose Hills.
Funeral corporations
rank tomb placement
by income bracket,
had her placed
in the middle layer.

With the proper prayers,
the Cambodian, Buddhist monks
harmonized their chants
before our final chance
to say our goodbyes.

Grey skies, sloped hillside.
Forecast expected rain,
but I still dropped
none.

I met my oldest mentor, Nature,
with tranquility under her caress
and tender hands.

Nature answered me,
embraced me,
with her warmth
of the cold.

Quarter

I hit quarter-life in January 2022,
but that's a survivor's saying.
They set the guideline that our hearts beat to 100.
What if I've already hit my mid-life
or final moments?

I think about how much time I've left,
but that number can't be measured
by the metric of age
as some people died
before they even lived.

We see how fickle life can be
when midwives sentence newborns to mid-lives.
You heard of the 18-year-old who spoke of conservation,
Now recall the ones who didn't make it past 11.

My type's independent of the month I was born.
Can't determine me by the category of Capricorn
with no astrology to define my personality.

I'm an MLK and Benjamin sandwich
for the day I evacuated the womb.
As I earlied to bed, I had a dream
that I'd be healthy, wealthy,
and late to the tomb.

We're born to die,
so give meaning to death.
Live on, give it all
until your final breath.

Another One for "god"

I'm sorry,

but I didn't attack you hard enough.

What an abusive relationship to say:
god loves us,
made us born sinners,
so that when we hate ourselves,
we'd have you to turn to.

you're cruel, birthed to be hateful
as a means to control "earthen vessels"
when we don't fit underneath the bar
and punished for being who we are.

your love is a poison
you put into our waters,
giving a dependable necessity
to rely solely on you.

I've no objection
against people who believe in you,
but those who speak for you,
lost rationality,
blinded by their faith in you.

I got folks who believe in me more than you do.
And my belief in them
is irregardless of their belief in you.
I can keep hating you,
but there's enough of that in this world.

How you justify love
being singular and not a spectrum,
you gave me a hard time trying to explain it,
yet you only have one definition.

I'm proud of this life of mine.
This journey I took gave me ambition,
for I can love myself just fine
without your permission.

A Sinister Propaganda

My fellow left-handed people
have been discriminated
throughout our history
by plague bearers of Christianity
who left behind all rationality.

When we adapted to a world
designed for the right in mind,
we acclimated to the tools
they have left us behind.

Ink applied to silver surfers on the pinky side.
Pulling away from the spiral binder to write
seemed like the only way that's right.
Coffee mugs shot our dexterity
when they deployed sinister strategy
with chemical burnings and shock therapy.

They defiled our hands
because we're defined
as devotees of their Devil
leaving us disheveled.

If you wondered why we pop up,
grow or "trend" our stray from majority,
think about how harder it is
to kill off the marginalized
in a more "accounted for" society.

This message ain't for the religious
who've learned from tragic history,
but to my fellow, friendly theists
equipped with kindness I can trust,
check up on your colleagues
blinded by senseless prejudice.

Here I do my due diligence,
as this issue is synonymous
for our diverse set of people
slain because they are atypical,
withdrawing off the norm category.

With this pen,
I write these words
with my left-hand
the right words
to have you left
on the right path.

I Am Autistic

There's no wrong mind
but a variant kind of thinking,
a deviant way of perceiving this world.

My ear's dyslexic,
but my attention's no deficit.
I lexi-jargon my own twists
to deliver my words.

I've cross-contaminated inputted intel
like crosswords cultivating my
internal black box to communicate
a culinary concoction.

I celebrate variant thinking
because neurodiversity
is no disability
but a different capability.

Don't believe the misinformed
who misinterpret
that we're the true culprit
as they confuse
high-functioning / low-functioning
with exceptional fun-ctioning
thought processing.

Believing we're defective
has a negative effect.
Our existence mislabeled
as entirely incorrect.

If you wonder how to treat autism,
just treat us
the way we want to be treated.

No ABA therapy, I see these ineffective ways
no matter what the ignorant says.
Autism doesnt speak for us,
just have an empathetic
and respectful method
we can trust.

I am who I am,
no cure for me to be fixed.
I am a software package
with a beautiful mind
blessed with gifts.

Accepting this trueness
within me is true power.
I'll resist against the currents
despite the voltage it brings.

It's shocking,
but I've been charged
with neurodivergence
since the beginning.

My Slanguage

My main slang splashed with Thai,
painted with Chinese genes in my blood.
Grew up in a Latino neighborhood,
raised by a Filipino community
who nurtured my artistic identity.

Southeast Asian accent layered by an Aspie cadence,
So-Cali swirl with a Valley style cherry
to top off the melted pot in my throat.

Languages are fascinating.
We all drink the same letters
but spit a plethora of remixes.

I'm multi-dipping in that hot pot with

my rooted tongue
branching to touch everyone.
You can stuff me in Filipino culture
I could tag along to
'cuz I'd not only stuff myself with Thai food.

My taste buds got taste, bud,
with stacks of spice on racks for seasoning
the flavorful connections,

because that diversity taste better
than flavorless vernaculars
stuck in monolinguals.

I'm a linguistics investigator, cultural connoisseur,
appreciator for dialects my mind's collected,
appropriate for cross-cultural celebration.

All the communities that raised me,
respective mentors that trained me,
gave me the unique language I speak
to create my slanguage of Chai-
                              nese.

Spelling My Name Correctly

chi (pronounced like "cheese" but without the "z" sound) *noun*,
: vital energy held to animate the body internally

chi•a (pronounced like "chi" above but followed by an "uh" sound) *noun*,
: an herb of the mint family native to Mexico and
Guatemala grown for seeds that can be eaten whole or used to make a
beverage

chi (pronounced like "Kyle" but without the "L" sound) *noun*,
: the 22nd letter of the Greek alphabet

chai (pronounced like "Chinese" but without the "knees") *noun*,
: a beverage that is a blend of black tea, honey, spices, and milk

Chai (pronounced and spelled unlike the first three definitions provided
in this piece, this word is pronounced and spelled EXACTLY like the chai
directly above that can also be seen on the menu of LITERALLY every
cafe that serves the simplest necessity to call themselves a working
cafe)
: the name of a guy who does a lot of stuff and drinks chai

My Voice

You are so interesting, but you don't talk much.

It's true, that compliment resonates,
frequented from other voices, but
I was raised
voiceless.

Talked over like my say didn't matter,
I felt ashamed I couldn't talk normal,
then I realized,

why would I want that?

My voice uniquely designed for me,
no one adverbial definition or speed
for when you hear my melody,
it sounds like no other.

My voice is a rhythm dancing
to no consistent beat per minute.

No formula to determine
the equation my cadence follows.

My voice plots on a graph
no regression line can analyze.

No chords in my puzzle box
with pieces fitting no size to conform
to a standard quadrilateral model.

No one to speak for me
but me.

You can try to imitate,
but you'll fall flat, still
it's flattery, I appreciate.

This voice is precious,
equipped only by me,
programmed interchangeable by choice.

It took a little while
but I found love
for my voice.

My Body

For a long time, it didn't make sense
how a healthy and abled body
could feel so ugly.

My body is a ruined temple
holding remnants in an unmarked forest
waiting to be raided.

I've told myself I was unattractive.
And it took one person to prove me wrong,
gently,
          continuously,

with laws of attraction,
positive affirmations repelled me
but negativity pushed me away

with every embrace of my lover's
arms, shoulders, heads
interlocking puzzled pieces
to fit upon one another
like a treasured chest
holding their weighted artifact
of a body.

But our body isn't quantifiable,
undefined by numbers on our scales,
weights we can press,
or the lengths of our reach.

It's qualitative,
defined by the scale of our love,
ways we press against pressure,

and the lengths of the journey
before we reach our destination.

We are blobs amorphous,
constant flux in stats composing us,
shapes undefined by societal standards
set for each of us
unique in our own ways.

No wrong body type,
Ain't nobody type out
our value for us.

True, it took validation.
Love and affection
from one to tell me,
I am enough,
affected my outgoing perception
of myself.

It took a little while,
through obstacles of the self
affirmations,
confidence,
esteem,

from another to love deeply,
unlock the gates of self-love
for my body.

My Name

The monks of the Wat Thai Temple
bestowed this name upon me.
It meant winner or champion.

What game was I playing to be called a winner?
The race game, game of life, genetic lottery?
Quite premature to be declaring victory
when my journey only just began.

I once thought about changing my name
to something colonized like Steve to fit in.
Now I'm blessed my name is a thirst
everyone can consume and take sips in.

My name is an amalgamation,
holding universes in the heads
of each person that has met me.

My name exists in fragments
building upon worlds in each mind
as they get to know the body this name occupies.

For when you hear my name,
you know a variation of what others
may recall from that name.

because my name...
my full name is

Sutichai Savathasuk

but you can call me

STEP XI: MR. CHAI TEA

I am the poet to my own muse, confused between the two.
I am two sides of an unstable coin, an agent of orderly chaos.
There's a method to my madness,
calculations in my improvisations.

A believer in the meaningless,
but our nothingness
to the universe
is everything
to our insignificance.

My tempo is sporadic, un-in tune with the beats of another.
Romanced the hell out of life, that beast of a lover.
No man's fella, but spaced out like no other.

Divided by none but mind,
undefined by function but passion,
fueled by fascination.

I am kinetic and potential, internalized, raw energy.
I am infinite in mortal shell
by all you see in me,
by all yet to be seen,
by all of which
I will be.

The 2nd Duodecennial

Through an azure fog, I glimpse my future distantly.
At 24, I look forward to 60, vacancy occupying certainty.
There stood a man fueled with passion and desire.

After I've dropped from the sky, dropped heartbeats
from murmurs in my words, throwing myself in
deep ends of oceans, flooded with hands raised high,

challenging hereafter's ambiguity requires being un-narrow-
minded, like a continuous chase / reaching for tomorrow.
Every yesterday's lack the knowledge I get, each day

becoming wiser, facing the unknown, standing tall,
braving to hold transparency in my actions for all.
My work is only beginning, priorities wildly out of order.

If opportunity gave me the translucent lens
to see through the veiled mist of my destiny
and predetermine the outcome to my future,

I wouldn't do it.

With steps I applied, existing in the present moment,
my end goal of success is only more worthwhile
compiling the blues of my art that healed my style.

Across time and space from me to him,
that old man can look back to my struggle's outcome
and bless the investment my inner child had grown.
I thank my mentors for giving the younger me
the choices my future self can appreciate
and be proud of the person I am today.

Success

It's an ongoing process,
this thing we call success.

Your life will be a sine wave,
the diverse elevation of L.A.,
but your value will never falter,
your time in this world only makes it grow taller.

Every mistake is a lesson learned.
Every hurt is a battle scar earned.

It's hard to see the progress you made
when it's all behind you.

But this rearview mirror gives time to reflect
that objects appear closer than you can see.

This life I painted on pages
is but one immortal project I've created.
Going from the next to the next,
that's succession.

When I slay my depression
over and over, is an eternal battle
that I win again and again.
Where each time it comes back to hit,
I hit harder,
and that's success.

Victory attained from the EXP gained
over the small battles of getting up
to the bigger wars
of keeping on.

Life begins with a single step,
not the first you take with your feet,
but the one you take with your breath.

I could die anytime
with a smile on my face
knowing that I've lived.

They say you die twice,
first in the grave,
second when your name disappears,
but the first is the one that matters.

The one where / I still
breathe in the air we share,
drink with the ones I care,
live with the ones who dare
me to jump off that cliff
as I lead us to adventure.

My FUN-eral

I.
I'd tell you not to cry at my funeral,
but are you going to let your life
be dictated by the dead?

Instead, I'd like you to feel
how you want to feel,
say what you want to say,
and really mean it.

Be honest to yourself and to me.
When you speak about our time
together, the memories flow naturally.

Feel happy, feel sorrow, feel optimistic,
feel grief, feel anger, feel thankful.
Feel free to express yourself

to let me know I was more than logic,
more than science, more than a brick
face but all the feelings you've emoted.

As I'm lowered in my grave,
a keen eye spots an inscription
on my coffin.

II.
The first clue to the treasures I've collected
in my lifetime. My final scheme to set
my still-alive friends on a wild adventure,

puzzles and mysteries
through riddles and poetry,
from hints obtained
by the knowledge of my history.

Setting course for my lads
to feel and fall for
every struggle I've been
through, to make it
to the end and find my hoard
deep in the chasms of the abyss

only to find
that the real treasure
is the friendships we made
along the way.

III.
Or some other generic inspirational
quote, I don't know.
Life is a tragedy.

Life can be cruel to not give me my way out.

Maybe, I won't die in a blaze of glory,
but from a cancer imbued
within me / the opportunity
to watch my friends go
on one last ride

from my real death bed
as I had set up a series of cameras
recording their journey
giving me the last spark of joy
before I pull the plug.

IV.
Or, Life is a comedy
of finishing my sentence
not with a comma
but with dramatic irony
by hypothermia.

V.
In my actual will,
please turn my body into a tree.

Thank you.

Museum of a Tea (Rex)

I am a museum.

Enter my grandiose entrance.
Before you stands my skeleton
of a dinosaur, chipped and worn
on scars from battles won.

My collagens touched by passerby
who pass through my directory.
So do the bones absorb oils
and become added to its history.

The paintings hung on walls
deliver you to another world
where each paint stroke
is speechless, breathing
words flying my true colors.

A gallery of photography
are memories of singular moments
feeding branches of outcomes
before their destinations.
What may come in the next frame
is open to your interpretation.

The botanical gardens hold
an exhibit for flora and fauna
of my travels, past
and future destinations.

This is no ordinary building.
The foundation of this infinite maze
builds additional wings
to its skeletal structure.

Messy, disorganized,
new finds as I find
more for me as you uncover
my buried treasures
in the back rooms.

This museum is a living organism
with you as the archeologist
of my remembrance
displaying my collection
of artifacts to the world
from your bookshelf.

Chai's Lessons

Judge a book by its cover.
The artist spent a lot of time
designing it to intrigue you,
but don't finish that thought
until you read it through.

We are three-dimensional characters
beyond the definement of our salary
our most outstanding quality,
or our romantic capability.

Everyone is more than their function in society,
no dollars to appraise values over another.

You can't capture the full picture of a person
from their religion, their sex, their design.
The spectrums imbued in each word
cultivated as you build upon their world.

We hear those who don't deserve the megaphone
when they confuse hate with freedom.
There's no counter to the freedom of speech
in a world with more ears than mouths,

but the ears don't give you your voice.

In a world of misinformation,
                     miscommunication,
                        misunderstandings,
it's okay to make mistakes.

Every mistake is a lesson,
and growth can't occur
if we alienate the imperfections
that make us human.

It is natural for people to make errors,
but it takes a braver soul to admit them.

How do you escape close-mindedness?

Well,

you open your mouth to create an argument;
you open your ears to begin discussion;
you open your mind to start a debate;
you open your heart to have empathy.

We're uniquely designed
with flaws and imperfection,
and our parent's faults
were only being human,
broken from the cycles
of trauma for generations.

Forgive, forgive, forgive, forgive.
Appreciate Life for giving us
the opportunity to return
the favors by letting go

hate in our hearts,
and embrace empathy,
change, and acceptance.
if your god can evolve
to become more welcoming,
then, we too, can resolve
our issues and learn.

We're boundless in our potential
to become more capable,
exploring as much as life can offer
to not be constricted to one label.

This world extends far
beyond our confinement;
our minds are containers
needing fulfillment.

You don't need to have joy to give it out.
There's more than enough for everyone.

Life is a playground,
so have fun.

To You

Well, traveler,

how else do I
put my heart on page,
transcribe 3D experience
onto 2D plane?

These archives are
a one-way street to get to you.
What words I've put here are
no more
than bits
of my mind,
scripted,
perfected
pieces of information.

I can spill my blood,
transfer that ink,
but I still carry
my DNA undried within.

At least
through these delicate pages
will some light bleed through,
revealed

through my writings,
the meaning of life
is to live it satisfactorily.
The expanse of one's stories
go beyond the surfaces of their skin.

Your omnipresence
through my journey
is a present to me.

And I thank you, reader,
for accompanying me
to this closure.

I can't predict the future,
but my adventure
is far from over.

Be you a future aspired,
untapped potential,
eloquent exceptional,
infinite unlabeled,
opulent spirit,
brave soul,
beloved unresentful,

there's no worthy destination
without the struggles of the journey;
there's no hands like yours
where this book would rather be.

As this epic comes to an end,
and the ink-stained tears fade,
I hope my history helped you,
for you now know

How Chai Tea is Made

Acknowledging My Road Map of Destiny

"No one is self-made. I put in the work, but it took a community to raise me."

Thank you, Hiram Sims of the Sims Library of Poetry, for fathering Community Literature Initiative (CLI) and encouraging writers to publish their stories, uplifting their voices to the world stage.

I'd like to acknowledge my season 9 CLIque Cal State LA chapter: Besskepp, Erica, Esteban, Gabe/Voth, Jim, Jane, Julia, Karo, Rosalilia, Wynter, and Tyler, under the guidance of our poetry teacher, Alex Petunia, for the work we put into our stories, and making this book a reality.

To Kuya Paul who bridged me to CLI from Palms Up Academy (PUA).

To Arianna Basco for mothering PUA, providing a supportive community that saved my life and nurtured my artistic growth at #RecessMic. I am forever grateful I found my family where I can be my authentic self and spew my chaotic, creative outlet to artists and dreamers of all sorts.

To Christian Perfas (Soul Stuf), who saw my potential at Sunday Jump (SJ) and brought me to PUA. Thank you for helping me find my tribe and being an awesome mentor to my continuously growing art skill.

To Ariel Jimenez, the truest, most supportive, empathetic homie, who invested in my self-worth and showed me what the world of arts is like.

To my blood family, with all the good stuff and tough stuff, who still support me in my artistic path (after being an engineer first).

To Chris, my childhood friend, whose wisdom and philosophy programmed my base structure for understanding and empathy. I'm thankful you were the positive influence in my youth, with our board games and escape rooms, logic puzzles and strategy discussions.

To the rest of the Foos: Gabrie, Yin, Jose, and David, whom I met at California State University, Northridge for engineering, for the wild road trips, reminding me that adventure is always out there.

To Jaclyn Lee Yangyuen (jly), for being the catalyst to unlocking my inner voice, and showing the possibility of the dual life of engineering / artistry.

Introduced by James Quan, who I've met through magic, mystery, and destiny.

Special Thanks

· To Bobbie Oliver at Tao Comedy Studio whose comedy class has incidentally taught me better public speaking than college courses by embracing the pause.

· To John Park who drew the sketches within these pages.

· To Ashley Lam who illustrated the drawings used for the chapter arts.

· To Nicholas Dobkin, who designed my book cover art.

· To Raelene Rizo for keeping me accountable, inspiring and loving me like no other.

AND TO Y'ALL!!

Wherever you may be, on your bed, on the train, on the bus, or in the public restroom, in your darkest nights, or underneath a tree, I acknowledge you. It means a lot to me that you've heard my story. Thank you.

NOTES

- "Free Fallin'", "Capturing the Moment", and "Quarter" published in Spectrum Online Edition: Last Hour on August 13, 2022

- "Why I Hike" published in Curious Nothing, 2023

- "A Letter from Prusa" is not an actual letter from Josef Prusa, CEO of the Prusa 3D-printers. Prusa is just what I decided to nickname my 3D-printer.

- "To The Foos" is dedicated to my road tripping buddies, with a pun on some U.S. National Parks we've been to and we've yet to go.

- "A Letter from Camille:" My aunt named her first car, Camille, after Claude Monet's wife. Camille would be passed to my grandpa and later be passed on to me.

- "To Palms Up Academy" features a pun on each person in the community on each line, along with the places we've had the privilege of calling our home: SIPA (Search to Involve Pilipino Americans), LACPA (Los Angeles College Prep Academy), KUMU Headquarters in Ktown, Robinson Space, and Lady B's humble abode.

- "Serial.println("Crush #1");" was inspired by my limited knowledge in Arduino-based coding from my Mechanical Engineering degree. To my Computer Science friends, the code is written for creative purposes only and cannot run. Please do not attempt to run the code. It does not work.

- "L.A. D.R.E.A.M." was inspired from Dyalekt of Pockets Change, a hybrid organization centered on financial literacy found at www.pocketschange.com

- "Nightmares of Relentless Torment" follows a series of nightmares I had during quarantine that I managed to write down before forgetting.

- "The 1st Duodecennial" and "The 2nd Duodecennial" were inspired by Arthur Wayu "Foundation" Kennedy's Five Duodecennials Project (an aspiration, a mentor, and a hunk of art)

Epilogue / Legacy

Oh, you're still here.
You know how _______________ you are
                    (adjective)

buying a(n) _______________ in this era.
                (noun)

Even going as far as reading past the poetry,
past the biography, and into this section here.
(unless you cheated and you just skipped to the end)

I _______________ the entire map of role–playing games,
   (verb)

as you found your way to this secret ending,
which is to say,
there is NO ENDING!

This journey continues.

Pass this _______________ along,
             (noun)

send it to a random address, or a friend, or a(n)

_______________ ,
   (animal)
or someone who needs _______________ .
                        (plural noun)

As we wander upon Nature's surfaces,
so, too, can this book,
along with our history, imprinting both of our writings.

Let's ________________ together!
        (verb)

I remember the ancient art of ______________ libs.
                                (emotion)

As the first to obtain this book, YOU get dibs
on how to fill in the ______________ .
                        (noun)

As scriptures become more and more digitized,
this physical copy
will be our ______________ !
            (¯_ (ツ)_/¯)

So, go ______________ !
        (emotion)

Imprint your tag upon this immortality project,
______________ a message for future travelers,
    (verb)
and, who knows, this book could end up at
______________'s
(famous person)

and they will see the ______________ ______________ we've
been through.   (adjective)   (noun)

Pass our history along
as our messages
traverse across
infinity!

About the Author

Sutichai (Chai) Savathasuk, or Mr. Chai Tea, is an autistic 3rd-generation Thai-American spoken-word artist from LA. With a background in Mechanical Engineering from California State University, Northridge, he blends comedy and poetry, captivating audiences with laughter and inspiration. A Sunday Jump and Palms Up Academy regular, Chai promotes empathy through his unique experiences as a nerd and adventurer, reminding us to find joy in our passions and seek connection. From mics to milk teas, hiking trails or board games, his enthusiasm for life shines through. You can find him at local boba shops and on Instagram: @mr.chai_tea.